M

The way we look

A FRAMEWORK FOR VISUAL ANALYSIS OF DRESS

The way

we look

A FRAMEWORK FOR VISUAL ANALYSIS OF DRESS

Marilyn Revell DeLong

 Iowa State University Press / **Ames**

Marilyn Revell DeLong is professor and director of graduate studies, Department of Design, Housing, and Apparel, University of Minnesota.

Composed by Iowa State University Press
Printed in the United States of America

First edition, 1987

Library of Congress Cataloging-in-Publication Data

DeLong, Marilyn Revell, 1939–
    The way we look.

    Bibliography: p.
    Includes index.
    1. Costume design.   2. Clothing and dress.
I. Title.
TT507.D46   1987   746.9′2   86–33769
ISBN 0–8138–1906–7

COVER: "Les Mannequins," 16″×18″ by Robert Hillestad is a textile collage of silk and metallic threads on a background of silk and wool reverse applique. It has been shown in numerous juried exhibitions and is represented in *Fiberart Design Book II*. Hillestad is a fiber artist and professor in the Department of Textiles, Clothing and Design, College of Home Economics, University of Nebraska-Lincoln.

Contents

Preface

THE reason for this book was summarized by a student upon completion of the course for which it was designed: to relieve tunnel vision. Both the author's research and teaching have helped in formulating the topics of the book. Students have had input throughout the entire process. Questions were asked and answered through long-term searching in the literature and through application of what was found. Even though references cited are few, they have been utilized, internalized, and applied.

The book format has been planned to encourage the viewing reference of the whole form. The first two chapters outline the concept and the ground rules required for application. The third chapter develops patterns of viewing the whole. Succeeding chapters discuss the visual relations that influence the whole, the definers and modifiers of visual parts. The visual form thus is investigated in terms of its potential visual relations and their interpretation, inherent in the context of the whole, the apparel-body construct. These visual relationships influence the process and the outcome of organizing, as discussed in chapter nine. The last chapter summarizes the approach and its usefulness in professions requiring the skills of the educated viewer.

Acknowledgments

THIS book could not have been formulated without the response of the students at the University of Minnesota. They helped me see what I did not see and let me know when they did not understand. In this way they helped apply the perceptual process to the visual form of dress—the apparel-body construct.

A special thank you to the reviewers of the manuscript. In its early stages reviewers were: Ann Marie Fiore, Edith Gazzuolo, Janet Hethorn, and Amy Searing. They had the ability to understand the big picture while responding chapter by chapter. In the later stages of review were Joanne Eicher and Robert Hillestad.

Many photographers and designers contributed their work for illustration. A special thank you to each of them for this major contribution to the book and for granting permission to use their work. Instrumental to the work of illustrating the book were Edith Gazzuolo, who helped to conceptualize visual materials, and Janet Hethorn and Bettie Minshall, who assisted with illustrations. A gift from Frances Henry helped with photographic expenses and allowed for some much needed experimentation. Many supporting resources came from the Department of Design, Housing, and Apparel at the Universty of Minnesota, the collections of the Goldstein Gallery, and the work of students of design. Also tapped were the resources of the Minneapolis College of Art and Design and of the University of Nebraska.

Finally for the personal support of Max and Tom, whose understanding and empathy never failed, thank you.

The way we look

A FRAMEWORK FOR VISUAL ANALYSIS OF DRESS

1

Educating vision

SEEING is often taken for granted as an innate ability. We make decisions of acceptance or rejection based upon conditioned visual responses. Thus this process is assumed to be beyond our control. But educating our vision is within our power. It is not a simple process, but we can become visually literate.

Visual literacy goes beyond merely seeing. It means understanding how we see visual forms and being able to share their meaning at some level of universality. It means reaching beyond our innate vision, beyond our intuitive capabilities to make instant visual decisions, and beyond our personal acceptances or rejections, which we call preferences˙and tastes.

Visual literacy offers the reward of understanding how we see and the effect of seeing. It offers an invitation to become less passive viewers of visual form, to be able to examine the nature of the whole as an interactive process. It offers an expansion of a viewer's understanding of visual form and an increased ability to achieve precise visual results. For a professional it offers the ability to know a broad range of visual forms and to communicate that knowledge.

Visual forms are those complex and interactive visual entities that we already know and take for granted. A visual form is that which we separate from our vision as meaningful—an object of our vision. The process of understanding visual forms can be applied to any visual form,

but the focus of this book is the *apparel-body construct* (ABC). The ABC is the visual form presented by the interaction of apparel on the human body; it is a construct or concept of a physical object based upon sensory data.

Understanding how we see and the effect of seeing is not beyond our control. But a methodology is needed to delineate the visual process—to observe the nature of the whole, to break it into visual units in order to study their makeup and interaction, and then to put them back together. Thus the methodology consists of observation of the whole, its subdivision into parts in order to become familiar with them, analysis of these parts as they relate to the whole, and interpretation of the whole as a fusion of ideas (fig. 1.1). The final step, evaluation, which concludes such a methodology, is quite different from quick judgments that are made, unconscious of the visual process.

Perceptive is a term used to describe

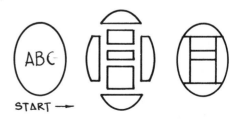

1.1. The method includes (1) observing the whole, (2) breaking it up and analyzing its visual units, and (3) reformulating the whole with a greater understanding of visual form.

3

persons who see well in the sense of taking in a given image—absorbing its colors, textures, placement in space, everything that contributes to its exact appearance. Some people do perceive more than others. These people have educated their vision. They understand more because they are constantly testing their reactions to what they see. They observe systematically and reason about what they see. Then vision becomes an active process. To educate vision, viewers need to consciously develop perceptual skills and be able to communicate their percepts through writing, drawing, and/or speaking.

Visual analysis of dress requires a well-developed ability to observe visual relationships and understand the associations necessary to interpret them. This book is intended to define, describe, and apply a vocabulary appropriate to understanding the visual effects of apparel on the human body. This is not a how-to book offering simple formulas for personal dressing. There are many such formula books, but they result in a limited view of the visual effect of the ABC rather than an expanded view of its infinite possibilities.

Who needs to develop perceptual skills? Perceptual skills are vital to the many professionals involved in clothing the human body—professionals involved throughout the spectrum of activities of designing, manufacturing, merchandising, and education.

To design an ABC or any one of its parts requires a careful consideration of the image of the whole. Thus a costume designer for the theater or a designer of apparel or accessories needs an expanded understanding of the potential of the ABC for visual effect. The accessory designer needs to consider not only the particular design of a belt but also the way that belt could be worn in the context of the whole. Designers need well-developed visual perceptual skills to understand the potential of their medium.

Those involved in the merchandising of apparel are interpreters of visual forms within our culture. Successful merchandisers consider how their audience will want to look and stock what their customers can wear to achieve that look. They display those images and realize the value of visually advertising the image. A fashion editor plays a parallel role of interpreter but verbalizes the visual forms of our time—communicating to others an analysis of trends. The merchandiser and fashion editor also need a highly developed sense of visual perception.

Other specialties rely particularly on the interpretation of the visual form of dress for personal appearance: the wardrobe consultant, the color analyst, the hair or body stylist. Their emergence indicates that there is an audience who wants help with their appearance. This audience recognizes and appreciates results but may not have the time, ability, or inclination to pursue the goal of optimizing the development of their appearance. This endeavor requires first the ability to observe and analyze visual forms and then to interpret them for specific persons and situations.

For too long, students have learned from an evaluative formula as a framework for understanding visual effect. Their aim has been to become sensitive to the visual form of dress without being able to analyze its visual effects. The framework offered here begins with observation, continues to analysis, and concludes with an interpretation and an evaluation of that form. This requires transcending a limited subjective viewpoint to become more objective and comprehensive in viewing. This systematic approach is ideal as a framework for educating oneself and others about the visual form of dress.

Perception—analytic vs. casual

To understand the apparel-body construct requires the development of analytical skills to perceive the visual relations inherent in that form: the whole and its parts, its images and ideas, and the way they are combined and interrelated. To do this requires an understanding of the perceptual process as an active and ongoing participation of the viewer with the visual form. Thus, in analytic perception one is absorbed in a search for form details and their relationship against an expanded context, the perspective of the entire form.

Casual perception arises from the necessities of day-to-day functioning. Much of our sensory experience is tied to what is needed to make sense out of our visual world, that is, the physical space around us. There is so much around us to see, hear, and touch that we have to be selective.

Ordinary perceptual activities are directed toward highlights and summary. We leave out or abbreviate rather than overload. In casual perception an individual is mostly interested in identification for action, and speed is an asset. In casual perception we do not necessarily analyze the perceptible features, such as color and shape, to draw conclusions. Casual perception will prevail if a conscious effort is not made to change the process.

Analytic perception aims at a systematic understanding of the form and its meanings. This includes all systematic attempts to observe, analyze, interpret, and finally evaluate the visual form of the ABC.

FORMATION OF A VISUAL RESPONSE. Analytic perception as a response to a visual form differs from casual perception in its goal. That goal is objectivity in our observation and analysis of form and can occur only when the viewer understands and experiences the three-way interaction of this response: (1) the visual form, (2) the situation of viewing, and (3) the viewer (interaction of viewer with form). Even though we can set aside or even ignore the influence of any one of these determinants for a time, each one's effects must be realized because our response is a result of all three.

FORM. Visual form is a structure of parts related to other parts and to the whole form. The visual form includes all that is directly perceptible: colors, textures, lines, and shapes and their formation into parts. Visual parts become the units of perception and they are affected by such modifiers as number, size, visual weight. The form also is influenced by expressive effect and culturally established meanings. The viewer interprets this meaning, which is directly or indirectly present in the form. Hard edges are perceived as different from soft edges, one shape as different from many, a vertical line as different from a horizontal line.

The form itself is a substantial factor in our perception. Whether the viewer is attracted by and then attends to it depends upon the visual structure and character of the form. The ABC as a form refers to the entire object. This includes its shapes and sizes, its textures and colors, and all materials arranged upon the body, such as cosmetics and shoes, and manipulations and modifications of the body, such as hair and body shaping. The term *apparel-body construct* is a reminder of the need for the viewer to take in all of these visual relationships.

SITUATION. The circumstances of viewing a form include both the immediately adjacent physical space as well as the broader cultural situation or social milieu. The immediate physical space includes the influence of other things in the field of vision, the surrounding area, the lighting, the neighboring objects. For example, a man in a black tuxedo would appear different in a well-lighted ballroom with many similar visual forms than he would coming toward you alone in the black of night. In a lighted ballroom the viewer is more aware of the silhouette as a hard edge defining the form. At night the silhouette edge would be less visible and for that reason and because of the white contrasting shirt the upper torso would become a viewing priority.

The broader cultural situation includes fashion trends and trends in tastes, values, and uses of the visual form. Even though a tuxedo is fairly constant through time, the experience of this form would vary depending upon the event. Since expectations of wearing are connected to events such as weddings, a viewer would be surprised to see a tuxedo in another situation. The viewer might pay more attention to the visual form—the man in the tuxedo—in an unexpected situation, such as in a grocery store, or try to place the form into an expected situation.

Other examples of the influence of situation on viewing can be cited. The view of ourself in a new clothing purchase while still at the store often differs markedly from our appearance in it after we arrive home. A viewer who has only recently discarded clothing as unfashionable has difficulty viewing it without emotional attachment. To view clothing more objectively as vintage dress is easier after a lapse of time.

VIEWER. The viewer has both unique-to-me qualities and experiences, as well as those shared with a social group. The viewer brings stable or slowly changing traits such as intelligence, personality, sex, physical stature, stage of maturation,

education, and special aptitudes as well as more rapidly changing traits such as interest and activity, likes and dislikes, mood, and expectations of the moment. How the form is interpreted is based upon previous experiences and present expectations as a viewer. For example, the viewer's own stature, age, and sex affect perceptual experiences through comparison with forms being viewed. Short viewers may experience tall ABCs differently when they compare size.

Thus the viewer possesses certain traits that are influential in the viewing process and their influence must be recognized. But there is a difference between understanding only one's own point of view and striving for more objectivity in viewing. To become visually literate, viewers must be able to question their viewpoint, testing it against reponses of others and realizing what portion of their response is individual and what is more universal. An analogy can be made to reading poetry. We can understand it because of our individual experiences, but hearing the interpretations of others can often illuminate the meaning even more.

The viewer who attends to visual forms organizes them based upon their form structure and meaning associations. The Gestalt psychologists recognized the extent to which the viewer automatically organizes what he sees. Since so much of ordinary viewing is performed on automatic pilot, the first need is for the viewer to begin looking at visual forms more critically, within an expanded framework that helps define the ABC beyond personal meaning.

Thus the three determinants—form, situation, and viewer—interrelate and influence each other. The immediate situation can influence a viewer as can the visual form. Seeing a visual form—a subject in a swimming suit on a beach—is different from seeing that same form in an office or on a stage. The visual form itself influences the mood set by the situation. A festive occasion is often more memorable to the viewer because of what was worn. Can you remember clothing worn in the past for a special event? Have you ever enjoyed anticipating and then seeing what people wore on a particular occasion?

Developing more objectivity

The viewer who begins to respond more systematically to visual forms is taking· the necessary first step toward more objectivity. This visual perspective is different from the perspective of the producer or the wearer, although each of these may benefit from this type of systematic viewing.

A producer is concerned with cost of manufacture, types of materials used, yardage needed, technique of assembling. The producer is concerned about the apparel after completion too, its position in the marketplace, how it compares with similar apparel in cost and quality.

As wearers, we evaluate dress for only a few people, ourselves and perhaps family and a few close friends. The basis of our perceptual experience is mostly intuitive. Sometimes we give advice to a friend that comes only from our subjective, wearer view. When asked our opinion of a color our friend wants to wear, we answer, "I enjoy wearing that color." If we answer from our subjective view, we may never think of the differences in personal coloring, never really see the friend in relation to that color. A more objective response to the friend might include answers to such questions as, Is that color good for you? How does it relate to your skin and hair color? Have you ever worn it before? How does it relate to other colors you wear? Do you like it?

A systematic response to any visual form requires practice and both time and attention. Adopting the observer view means becoming more comprehensive in our viewing. Initially we need to overcome viewing habits in which we make instant judgments, unaware of the connection of the form to its meaning.

INFLUENCE OF VIEWING HABITS. Our viewing habits and the necessities of ordinary perception allow us to function on a day-to-day basis. Since seeing takes time and effort, we develop shortcuts for seeing those objects and events that we fully expect. They often don't register in our consciousness. We do not need to be aware of much that is around us to carry out many life events (fig. 1.2). Selective

1.2. Selective attention allows us to see what we are searching for—the time, a theater, or transportation.

attention provides only the information we need. Think about how little we see as we drive down a familiar road. Only an unexpected event or object will sharpen our awareness and cause us to examine the scene in detail.

We don't examine in detail if a cue will allow a shortcut. Only when the cue doesn't work do we sharpen our awareness. We unconsciously perceive many associations related to the ABC. Thus, during the unisex movement when cues for maleness and femaleness became blurred, many viewers became aware of the need for more distinctive cues.

How we make sense out of the world grows from our personal experiences developing within a given society. These experiences help us set priorities on what to look at, what to attend to, and how we attend. By the time we reach maturity, our habits of sensory selection may have greatly reduced our ability or motivation to experience openly. We have developed tunnel vision.

We are all at various stages in the development of our perceptual skills. Along the way, we may have developed a certain way of looking at a form and thus a favored frame of reference for viewing. We often look at our world through our current glasses, be they rose colored or blue toned or textured. We then respond from this perspective: This is my favorite color! or I love texture! Our tendency is to fix our perceptual framework and look at forms within that framework. This deters us from seeing all there is, especially if our expectations are met. With practice, however, an active discovery attitude can be substituted for a passive or reactive one.

In the field of fashion apparel new forms are continually being presented for viewing consideration. Many who need to, have not trained themselves to perceive and interpret new visual experiences. By broadening our viewing ref-

erence to include unfamiliar forms, we will be able to respond actively and openly to new forms. New ways of looking at forms will become customary. A viewer who is looking for a variety of cues is more likely to find them.

To understand the perspective of a particular visual form requires careful observation of a range of visual forms. At first it may be easier to view unfamiliar forms in order to understand the range of visual possibilities, and eventually the more familiar forms can be placed into this perspective. Flexibility in viewing is a by-product of subjecting oneself to a great variety of visual forms.

A "what if" attitude helps in adopting an experimental approach. This is the ability to visualize or imagine substitutions. For example, What would happen if this color were to be substituted for that? What would the difference be? What changes in viewing would occur?

INFLUENCE OF ASSOCIATED JUDGMENTS.
Under most circumstances our ability to make quick visual decisions is very useful; in fact it is part of our survival. But observers sometimes make judgments without understanding what they see. Sometimes they remember only whether or not they liked it. Some observe only what they like. When clothing is viewed only to express a personal preference, an objective analysis of its visual effect is not always necessary.

Liking can even become a prerequisite to any further experience. For example, a fabric given to a student of design with the goal of imagining and developing alternative plans for its use may elicit a response such as, How can I work with this? I do not like the fabric! An affinity for the fabric may indeed have helped the imagining process, but it need not be such a delimiting factor.

Even though we sometimes reduce what we see to what we evaluate favorably, we can make this habit work for us by making it a conscious act. This means finding a way to become aware of an essentially unconscious act, to recognize the basis for our judgments—why we like or dislike an object. If we learn to suspend normative judgments, or opinions, we can develop a very useful ability—to see with a more open mind.

Educating vision to take an objective point of view means learning to see before we judge. This is not to say judgment is to be ignored, only laid aside temporarily. Our aim is not to change judgment but to back it with understanding and to develop our ability to consider those objects we do not immediately favor. We can learn to separate our judgment of forms from our ability to analyze them. In an attempt to suspend judgment, it helps to express immediate feelings of like or dislike, ranging from boredom or mild interest to intense excitement. This not only puts these feelings into perspective, but eventually they become more varied. Suspending judgment to develop our perceptual abilities will allow for separating types of "wow" or "nice."

INFLUENCE OF ASSOCIATED MEANINGS. Perception of the ABC is fraught with meanings. These range from associations of the direct sensory experience of the form—This is red and looks exciting—to more abstract associations, which require reference to the time and place in which we live—This looks like a new trend. But the viewer must extend beyond meaning to consider its relation to form itself. We do associate meaning with visual forms, their potential for satisfying possibilities and for having consequences of action centered upon them. Even though surfaces and shapes are automatically perceived as shoes, fur, apples, and people, our responses are specific to the contour, shape, size, color,

and motion of objects and we do not confuse a shirt and an apple, neither do we need to see their form in any detail to make this association.

The relation of concrete details of visual forms, i.e, their surfaces, edges, and spaces, to meaning is a vital one to understand. Many examples illustrate the connections of meaning with specific surfaces, edges, and motions. For example, *youth* may call to mind smooth textures, bright colors, and activity.

Meaning associations need to be considered in the process of learning about and interpreting visual forms. Associations can be simple when directed to identification of apparel, for example, *blazer* refers to a type of covering for the upper torso with specific lines and shapes. But associations can be complex in the connection between the concrete form and the symbolic. The name John Wayne calls to mind a specific configuration that broadly includes aggressive posturing, speaking, as well as a certain type of clothing.

To develop more comprehension of the visual form, the relation of form and meaning needs to be understood. This may require separation of the two elements at first. Then their interrelation can be heightened.

An approach and focus

The purpose of this book is to develop a framework for analyzing and interpreting visual relationships of the body in dress. The goals are to perceive from an observer point of view, to think visually, to expand the visual processes by sharpening our awareness of the visual form of the clothed body. A means will be presented to develop an investigative attitude about factors that can affect perception of the ABC. This will be accomplished by presenting a language for visual analysis and exeriences that will aid in developing an ability to image in visual terms.

The nature of this language is important in fostering an investigative attitude. Vocabulary that is too subjective can modify viewing. The language introduced in this book is intended to cause us to set aside quick judgments, allowing us to observe, analyze, and interpret the visual form of the ABC. At the end of each chapter in the "Visual Exercises" section, focused visual experiences apply the vocabulary and offer a means to personal involvement with the material. By opening our awareness, we may better understand the complexities of the visual form of dress, which is the integration of the body structure with the selection and structuring of materials.

TAKING THE OBSERVER VIEW. By now you as the observer are more aware of what is meant by taking the observer point of view. Let us review some of the ground rules.

First, we are taking the point of view of the observer of the ABC. We are not considering apparel from the point of view of the wearer, the person inside the clothing, although ultimately this view will be better understood. Therefore, the observer is interacting with the ABC not as one person to another but as a viewer trying to discover something of its visual effect, to understand it as a visual phenomenon.

The ABC is separated enough from the viewer to be considered a visual form or organization in space. This means the ABC is either far enough away from the viewer to be seen entirely from one reference point or the viewer is looking at himself or herself in a mirror.

Thus, in order to understand the visual organization of the ABC as a physical entity, for a brief time we must suspend subjective judgment and separate our-selves from interpersonal interactions that could take place. This is a way to objectify what we are viewing. In no way are we denying the humanness of the person in the clothing. We are concentrating for a time on literal viewing and the visual interactions that can occur if we allow ourselves time, curiosity, and some distance from the ABC. Then a method of systematic viewing can be introduced that will help us to become more discriminating viewers of the ABC.

Visual exercises

I. Understanding individual and group response to the ABC.

When comparing several apparel-body constructs it is useful to begin by analyzing the effect of the whole image and then to proceed to analyze what has caused this effect. To analyze the whole effect a recording of your spontaneous reaction is useful.

Activities A, B, and C are to be completed individually.

A. Five numbered photos of contemporary ABCs will be given to you.[1] Place each one's number on each line below in a position between the two extremes (midpoint on the line represents neutral).

like_____|_____	dislike
attractive_____|_____	unattractive
youthful_____|_____	mature
calm_____|_____	exciting
simple_____|_____	complex
fashionable_____|_____	unfashionable
sophisticated_____|_____	naive
romantic_____|_____	classic
happy_____|_____	sad
modest_____|_____	immodest
serious_____|_____	fun

---

1. *Teacher Note:* Divide the class into groups of five or six. Select groups of five photographs from current magazines or catalogs. Each group of photographs should consist of colored, full-length, and clear images of persons of similar age and gender, varying in visual effect (e.g., all adult males, some in business suits and some in casual clothing). The photos can be passed within each group to complete the word pairs in Part A.

business_____	|	_____pleasure
sexy_____	|	_____unsexy
formal_____	|	_____casual
one occasion_____	|	_____many occasions
organized_____	|	_____unorganized
defined surfaces_____	|	_____ambiguous surfaces
bold_____	|	_____subtle
one focal point_____	|	_____many focal points
moving_____	|	_____still
heavy_____	|	_____light
loose_____	|	_____fitted
light_____	|	_____dark
colorful_____	|	_____neutral
flowing_____	|	_____stiff
crisp_____	|	_____soft
bright_____	|	_____pale
flat_____	|	_____textured
horizontal_____	|	_____vertical
blend_____	|	_____contrast

B. Can you think of any other word pairs that would describe the ABCs? List them.

C. Now go through the word pairs. Note which numbers are placed together on a line and which, if any, are at the extreme positions. Write comments about observations.

D. When activities A–C have been completed, compare observations with the rest of your group. This may best be accomplished by comparing with one person and then discussing with the entire group. Briefly write your observations of the similarities and differences in position of numbers after comparing responses.

II. Communicating the visual form through verbal description.

The purpose of this exercise is to examine the ease or difficulty encountered when translating visual images into verbal descriptions and vice versa. The verbal language we use to describe visual forms ranges in degree of complexity from simple, commonly understood terms to more specific terminology. When communicating information verbally about a visual form, the abilities of both the sender and receiver to express themselves and to interpret what they read or hear may be related to their ability to translate verbal information into a mental, visual image. Developing this ability provides a challenge for individuals such as advertising copywriters, fashion editors, buyers. Further, they need to describe visual forms in a manner suitable for their audience. In order to do this, they need to know what terminology provides the best visual image for the receiver to successfully interpret the visual form.

For this exercise you will need to select a partner and work with him or her.

A. During this part of the exercise, each person will be working as a describer of a clothing ensemble.
1. Select one photograph of a clothing ensemble from a current magazine or catalog. (Note: Do not allow your partner to see the photograph.)
2. Complete the following ensemble description, keeping in mind that the receiver will have only your words from which to form a mental image.
   a. Description of main parts and function in the ensemble.
   b. Description of line, shape, color, and texture.
   c. Possible associated meanings.
3. Exchange descriptions with partner. You will now become a receiver and should follow the receiver guidelines in B.

B. During this part of the exercise, each person will be working as a receiver of a clothing ensemble.
1. Using only the written description, form a mental image of the clothing ensemble. Form as complete an image as possible and mentally record it. (Note: If helpful or necessary, you may use sketches to illustrate your mental image.)
2. Is the information presented sufficient for you to form a mental image? If not, what additional information do you require?
3. Obtain the photograph of the ensemble from your partner and compare it with your mental image. Record how accurate your image was and what similarities or dissimilarities occurred.

C. Discussion and analysis.
1. Discuss with your partner the effectiveness of his/her description in assisting your formation of the visual image.
2. From your discussion write an

analysis of why the language used in the ensemble description you wrote was effective or ineffective in communicating a visual form.

III. Relating perception and preference of visual form to exposure over time.

Amount of exposure to visual material may affect what we see or don't see as well as what we like or don't like. The following exercise may help you become more aware of the process and results of increasing familiarity with selected photographs of the apparel-body construct.

A. Collect several photographs of apparel-body constructs from magazines, newspapers, or catalogs, choosing as varied an array as you can and including ones you like and ones you dislike.

B. Taking one photograph at a time, glance at it and put it out of sight. Write down the main emphasis of the photo and everything else you noticed about it. Include your preferences.

C. Again taking one photo at a time, look at it for 3–5 minutes, then put it away and note what you saw.

D. Pin up the photos in your home or place of work, in a spot where you will happen to look at them often (e.g., above your desk, at waist level in the bathroom). Leave them up for a week. Then, for each one, write down what you saw and whether you like or dislike it.

E. Were there any differences in what you saw each time you observed and wrote? Did you notice more or less about any of the photos over time? Did your preferences concerning any of the photos change?

Can you group photos for which your response was similar? For which your response changed in the same way? What about these photos is similar?

Can you draw any conclusions from this exercise? Write them down. Can you relate your experience in any way to the way you experience new styles on the market? Changes in your own or others' looks? Anything else?

A variation of this exercise might involve choosing photos to represent the concepts of youth or maturity and afterwards analyzing each for degree of simplicity-complexity, boldness-subtlety, and appreciation over time. Arrange the photos on a continuum and compare.

2

A systematic approach to viewing the form

IN the first chapter emphasis was on visual response as an interaction of observer, the form, and the circumstances of viewing. The observer needs to be engaged in systematic viewing, which is an active, seeking process. Now the question is, What is systematic viewing of a visual form? The objective of this chapter is to introduce a process and to discuss what it means to view the form of the apparel-body construct (ABC).

First we will look at an approach or a system of viewing. Above all, we need a system that offers a repeatable process and a definable language. The viewer who proceeds through the system enough times with enough visual forms can begin to place one visual form into a spectrum of visual forms. Beginning with one ABC, the goal is to understand it as an entity but also to understand its place within a defined set of polarities that identify extreme forms. Then the viewer, using the system, will fill in the range of forms within the extreme forms (identified in chap. 3).

The visual form has a structure made up of perceptible attributes and visual parts within a whole, which can lead the viewer. The viewer's role is to become absorbed in the process of viewing the form structure, understanding the relationship of parts within the whole. The form does not always lead the viewer throughout the entire ABC; therefore the viewer must consciously keep referring to the whole.

The viewer who maintains an analytic approach to visual forms develops and builds on an understanding of a spectrum of forms. This viewer can begin an informational bank of visual forms, which continues to become more complete with use. The viewer also can begin to verbally document what he views. Eventually the analytic viewer who persists can acquire a well-developed perceptual ability, the ability to observe and understand the ABC and its visual relations.

Steps in the perceptual process

A systematic approach is necessary to the development of those perceptual skills that will lead to a more discriminating response. The viewer must concentrate for a time on literal viewing of what is objectively present in the visual form. In doing this the viewer will develop a different kind of awareness of visual form. The process is introduced here but is expanded in chapter 10.

A systematic approach involves a conscious effort to detach ourselves from our own self-interest and viewpoint. This means setting aside our person-to-person interactions. This detachment also requires enough distance from the form to examine it and enough time and atten-

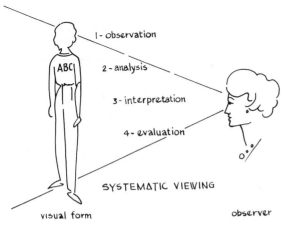

I - observation

2 - analysis

3 - interpretation

4 - evaluation

SYSTEMATIC VIEWING

visual form

observer

2.1. Steps in the perceptual process of viewing the apparel-body construct.

tion for viewing. The viewer is forced to pause and view not only the conspicuous features but also the less conspicuous ones, thereby preventing misunderstanding of the function of the parts and the ordering of the whole.

The process begins with observation of the visual form, including attention to the form in its entirety. The next step, analysis, requires a thorough consideration of the visual relations—how each part influences the other parts and the whole. The third step, interpretation, consists of looking for the visual relationships and associations of meaning that seem to summarize and explain the form. The fourth and final step, evaluation, concludes and builds upon the other three (fig. 2.1).

To proceed, select an entire visual form for study or select two that upon first inspection appear quite different. This means the form is in full view and needs to be stationary for sufficient time to follow the procedure. A clear colored photo from a magazine is a good place to start. After selection proceed with the four steps.

OBSERVATION: ATTENDING TO THE FORM. In this step the goal is to observe and describe what is immediately apparent

in the ABC as a whole. Note descriptive information that accompanies the photo. If more than one form is used, a comparison can be helpful.

Experience the entire form as a whole. How much space does it occupy? Observe the silhouette. Does it flare outward from the body? Is it defined distinctly or indistinctly? Is it easy to view? Does the ABC appear to come forward or to remain in the background? Is your eye directed throughout the form or does it remain in one area?

Do you notice lines and shapes? Are edges distinct or subtle? Are there few or many? Where are they located? Do you notice surfaces? If so, do you notice colors, textures? Is there a play of light and shadow on the surface? Does the surface appear flat or rounded? Does it appear to be thick or thin? Do you notice the body or the clothes? How do they interact?

The vocabulary is important in such an account. Use descriptive rather than evaluative language. Label a shape rectangular or oval rather than lovely or grotesque, the edge of a contour sharp or indistinct rather than harsh or harmonious. In this way you can describe without reflecting your own value judgments.

In figure 2.2 the three ABCs occupy approximately the same amount of space. The silhouette is more distinctly defined in figure 2.2a and the eye is directed to this edge. The surfaces appear relatively flat. Thus this ABC is viewed as a whole. Then the contrast at the neck is noticed. In figure 2.2b surfaces appear more rounded and edges are more subtle. This ABC is viewed as a whole. In figure 2.2c the silhouette is noticed less than the interior shapes in the upper and lower torso.

ANALYSIS: CONSIDERING THE RELATIONSHIPS. In this step the structure is examined, that is, the whole is divided into

a   b   c

2.2. Comparing three similar ABCs aids the description process. *Photos courtesy of Donaldsons, Minneapolis, Minnesota.*

its visual parts. Cover the photo with tracing paper to remove value contrast and quickly trace lines and shapes, approximating details. After identification of the parts, the concern is the influence of one part on another and how the parts affect viewing of the whole.

What separates from the whole for attention? How many separate parts are there? Which parts are noticed first? Number the parts in the order in which they are viewed.

Examine the parts as they separated from the whole. Consider why you were attracted first to part number l, second to number 2, and so forth. How does each part relate to the whole form—by color, texture, size?

Examine the part-to-whole relation. How do the parts function within the form? Are they repetitious and regular or irregular and singular? What influence does line, shape, color, or texture have on the viewer? Describe their use in the

form and how this affects viewing. A description should be as complete and objective as possible, such that another observer could agree with the account.

In figure 2.2a the ABC is viewed as a whole first. Then the contrast of light value at the neck and the contrast between skin and hair attract attention. The light value of this one dominant area is repeated in the cuffs at the wrists, but their smaller areas make these parts less dominant. The shape of the hair encloses the head as the suit does the body. In 2.2b the whole is viewed first but for a different reason. The surfaces of the jacket and skirt and hair are noticed more because of the texture variation and the play of light and shadow. The value relationship between the blouse and suit is less contrasting than in 2.2a. The briefcase is a more contrasting part. The shape of the hair is more irregular and open to the surround than that in 2.2a. In figure 2.2c the viewer notices parts first, the dominant geometric lines of the skirt and the repetition of these values in the flower motif at the upper torso and in the skin and hair. Another focus after viewing these parts is the lighter value of the shirt collar and cuff. The head shape is in contrast with the horizontal line at the shoulders and can be grouped with the focus at center front.

INTERPRETATION: SUMMARIZING THE FORM.
The goal of interpretation is to look for the relationships and associations that summarize and explain the form. Here individual interpretations are compared with those shared with others. What are the visual relationships that become priorities as observed in the form? What seems to fuse as the pervasive and connecting linkage? This step must build upon the preceding steps.

Does an idea, or concept, seem to connect the parts of the form? First, record all word associations that come to mind. As you begin, consider all alternatives without judgment. Complete the sentences: This reminds me of . . . This looks like . . .

Now consider your first impressions made without judgment. Which seem to be possible and probable? Step back from the visual evidence as noted and consider what within the culture is valued and of high priority. Does the form relate to this in any way? Test your impressions on others and formulate what you believe to be the main message of the ABC.

For example, the viewer could comment and then begin interpretation in this way: Figure 2.2a looks like a judge, someone with authority, or a high-powered executive in a business suit. An interpretation could then include the solid, dark figure as defined by edge. Flat surfaces attract immediate attention and present a focus at the head and neck.

Figure 2.2b looks softer, more approachable, friendly—a saleswoman perhaps or someone who meets lots of people. The middle value of the suit surfaces carries light and shadow and more parts are perceived, although the ABC can be viewed first as a whole. Figure 2.2c looks more casual, as do coordinated separates for a social event. Here the parts dominate and although there is a visual connection between them, they are viewed first as discrete. Perhaps the casual interpretation is partly because of these independent parts.

EVALUATION: CONSIDERING THE VISUAL MERIT. Evaluation needs to be postponed until each of the other steps of the process has been completed. Much can be overlooked in reaching a conclusion when evaluation is not preceded by careful observation, analysis, and interpretation.

Consider the visual merit of the form. A comparison with other known forms helps evaluation. To evaluate visual merit, consider such criteria as the following: Did the ABC attract your attention? Did it hold your attention? How does it rank with similar forms? Is it unique in conveying visual relationships or messages?

Other evaluative criteria need to be specified, such as, Is the message of the form congruous or mixed? Is it consistent with other forms of the designer or manufacturer? Is it acceptable, desirable, to a large diverse audience, a small select audience? How does it express the period in which it was created?

Figure 2.2a might be evaluated as attracting attention because of the dark value of surfaces and the distinct edges. Although the form is typical of the authoritative business suit, the fuller skirt softens its otherwise closed nature. The focus at the neck is also hard edged but subtle. A more typical treatment would be a tie or scarf with a pattern such as a stripe. Figure 2.2b attracts less attention as an ABC because of the softened edges of the silhouette. The form appears more open to the surroundings and even though it is still a suit, it is not as dominating as the suit in 2.2a. The nuance of the surfaces are played out and make this ABC easy to view. The stripes that appear when the skirt is moving help to sustain attention. Figure 2.2c attracts attention to the interior by use of similar values and more independent parts in the upper and lower torso. This suit is more playful and perhaps more unique as a suit. The ABC still appears to be ordered but in a more random manner. The three suits could be worn for different purposes as indicated in the interpretation.

The visual form

Visual form has been defined as a distinctive arrangement of surfaces, lines, and shapes. To describe a form, we traditionally delineate its features, its particular lines, shapes, colors, and textures. This is necessary to our understanding, but the term *form* actually refers to the entire object. In the case of the apparel-body construct, we need to develop a frame of reference to consider this in its entirety (refer to section on form, chap.1, for discussion).

Use of the term apparel-body construct will reinforce the need to include all the visual relationships—within the form and between the form and the surrounding space. What is put on the body can be viewed as separate and apart from it or as integral with it, depending upon whether the relationship is one of contrast or of similarity. The surrounding space affects the viewing of the form, but again we rarely consider its influence. If taking note of all of the visual relation-

ships of the ABC is not a viewing habit, learning to do so will require a conscious effort.

Visual relations of the ABC

Relationships are the connecting links between similar or different features by which the viewer perceives the visual form, the ABC, as an organization. We connect the features that are similar in such qualities as hue, texture, shape and in such quantities as size of area, value of color, length and movement in line. The frame of reference for viewing is simply the arrangement of the whole and its parts, incorporating all these visual relationships.

Features of the form can be viewed separately, but their significance is also dependent upon their relation to the whole. The Gestalt psychologists stated that the whole is more than the sum of its parts. The viewer can only fully understand color or line or any of the separate features by considering them in a particular instance, a particular whole. For example, imagine a sweater differing in only one feature from another sweater. A difference in color may influence not only perception of surface. A viewer may also relate the sweater in a very different way within the ABC.

An understanding of the form includes an awareness of the interaction of clothing features with body features (e.g., the influence of location of the clothing on the body). It helps to envision the effect of one item in its relation to others by putting them all on and looking in a mirror or laying them out as they would be positioned on the body. The selection of a belt for a specific visual effect provides an example. The belt can be considered in combination with other items to be worn, such as shoes and trousers. The viewer needs to consider how the belt will be viewed, as a focal point or as a background item; the placement of the belt; its color, size, texture as related to the body.

Gestalt psychologists have identified two very basic processes used in organizing a form—grouping and segregating. The processes of grouping and segregating are viewer activities focused on the way the form is arranged. They are based on the premise that the viewer strives to perceive order at its most simple level—where most visual meaning occurs. Meaning here refers to that which is directly perceptible in the form. Grouping is what the viewer does when similar visual units will be simpler to see or make more sense grouped or considered together. Segregating occurs when the viewer separates two unlike visual units. These processes are important in forming visual relationships (fig. 2.3a).

Both processes, grouping and segregating, occur constantly for the viewer. The viewer does not have to be conscious of grouping and segregating for them to occur, but bringing them to consciousness is necessary in order to understand viewer response. When the viewer focuses on a visual point or area, grouping and segregating can be taking place simultaneously. A visual part can be viewed as a grouping that is separated from what surrounds it. For example, if the viewer focuses on three buttons in a row on a sleeve, grouping of the three buttons occurs at the same time that the buttons are segregated for viewing from the remainder of the sleeve.

Perceiving a visual form is a repeated scanning-focusing process. What we focus on depends on the form and its specific attributes. Visual relationships affect the viewer by directing movement. A visual unit that separates from the whole is a source of focus and pause.

Visual relations result from comparisons of sensory attributes. For example, hues can be presented in a natural array of yellows grading into oranges, then reds, purples, blues, and greens, coming full circle back to yellow. In this order a sensory scheme of closely related hues is presented. Hues viewed together that are out of this order, such as red and green, produce a contrast effect (fig. 2.3b).

Sensory relations occur within a specific attribute. Textures can be rough or smooth, lines can be straight or curved. *Gradation* is a term used for a series of barely perceptible steps in a sensory scheme of color, texture, or line. A sensory contrast occurs when there is a gap in presenting the scheme. A relationship based upon a gradation might include that of shapes varying in measurable quantity—in size, in value, in number. The viewer reads these relationships,

A { GROUPING - similar visual units
    SEGREGATING - unlike visual units

2.3. Visual relations that influence the viewer's perception of the ABC.

B { SENSORY SCHEMES -

	SIZE	VALUE	DENSITY	LINE
gradation	○○○∘	■▨□		I(⟨⟨c
contrast	○∘	■□		III c

and their location within the ABC influences direction of the viewing path (fig. 2.4).

2.4. An ABC with both gradation and contrast of value directs the viewer vertically. Gradation occurs between the upper and lower torso; contrast occurs at neckline and shoes. *Photo courtesy of Donaldsons, Minneapolis, Minnesota.*

Thus, there are relations of grouping and segregating, contrast and blending (degrees of gradation) within the form. As stated previously, these can occur between the entire form (the ABC) and the immediately surrounding space, between the clothing and the body, and between the units of the clothing ensemble. Again, to consider the extent of the possible relations, the viewer must adopt as frame of reference the form in its entirety (fig. 2.5).

THE ABC AND ITS SURROUNDING SPACE. The first visual relationship to keep in mind while viewing the ABC is the one with the immediately adjacent surround.

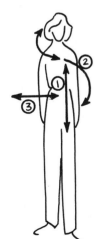

① within apparel

② apparel - body

③ ABC - surround

2.5. (drawing). ABC relationships fall into three categories. (photo). In a comparison of the left and right ABCs as to *ABC-surround,* the left figure presents a more contrasting outline, hard edge with the surround, than does the right figure, which is more similar in value to the surround. In an *apparel-body* comparison the left ABC is more contrasting than the right in value of apparel and body coloring. There is a similarity in the shape of hair and necklace in the left ABC and similarity of texture of hair and sweater vest in the right ABC. A *within apparel* comparison shows more contrast in the surface textures of the ABC on the right. The vertical emphasis of both ABCs is accomplished by the continuation of the line of the pants into the upper torso. *Photo courtesy of Donaldsons, Minneapolis, Minnesota.*

Understanding the ABC involves observing how the surrounding area affects it. This spatial orientation of the ABC is perhaps the most difficult of the three relationships to keep in mind. At first it may seem unnatural since we must scan the outline, or silhouette, to perceive it. This scanning also requires observing the adjacent area because of its effect on the definition of boundary. For example, a mostly white ABC would have a different sort of boundary—and therefore visual impact—when the space surrounding it was white as opposed to a contrast such as green or black.

Much of the visual impact of the ABC at a distance derives from the frame created by the silhouette. The ABC can be visually separated from the immediate background or can seem to blend with the space around. A boundary can also seem to disappear at times. If the ABC is viewed as separated from adjacent space, it must have distinct boundaries, or edges. The difference in viewing a visually distinct versus an indistinct silhouette is the result of the relation of the ABC to the space around it. Either the form or the space can be manipulated, although we usually perceive a distinct edge to be the result of the surfaces of the ABC and not of the character of the surrounding space.

This surrounding space is more or less controlled or controllable in a photograph or other staging of the ABC. In everyday situations the surround is not controlled, but the ABC can be considered as it would be in its most likely setting. For example, the dark business suit with its straight and vertical lines usually has a defined, hard-edged boundary, or silhouette. The typical surrounding space is a light-to-medium value and this provides enough of a contrast to create a distinct silhouette most of the time. The silhouette of a dark-value ski suit, however, might look quite different on a

snowy slope from how it looks in a darkened ski lodge lit only by a fire. In the former instance the silhouette is a sharply defined boundary against the snow, and in the latter, softened and perhaps even blurred and indistinguishable at times.

THE CLOTHING AND THE BODY. The surfaces placed upon the body can interact with the body structure. The surfaces can visually unite with body parts or segregate them. A neckline could be similar to the width of the head and create a continuous line relation. A honey blonde hair color can blend with a jacket of similar hue and value, creating a grouping through color. A white satin shirt adjacent to dark, curly hair and brown skin would offer contrast both in texture and value, thus segregating a part of the body from the surface of the shirt.

A sensitivity to the interactions taking place between body and clothing can be encouraged. Test yours. A black dress will not look the same next to different body colors. On a black-haired, light-skinned model the surfaces of hair and dress would be similar in hue and value. If black hair is shiny and next to a matte surface of the dress, we would view a soft edge between the two different textures. The first focus would likely be the silhouette of the ABC, which would offer a continuous and defined boundary, or the face by contrast of skin with hair and dress. On a blonde with golden hair and skin, the same black dress would contrast. A distinct visual part would be created by the hue and value in hair and skin color.

THE CLOTHING ENSEMBLE. There are many potential visual relationships within the clothing ensemble. Surfaces can be related by hue, value, intensity. Textures can be similar in roughness or smoothness, crispness or softness. Some surface qualities affect the shapes and the way the light and shadows can play on the surfaces. For example, middle values tend to carry light and shadow effects much better than dark values. Clothing shapes include collars, sleeves, cuffs, the silhouette, the upper torso and lower torso, shapes created by the play of light and shadow on pleats and gathers. These shapes can be related in their angularity, their roundness, their size, direction, or location on the body.

The colors, textures, lines, and shapes of clothing can group or segregate. An example of grouping would be six buttons spaced close to center front in two three-button rows. They can appear to group as a rectangular shape or, depending upon the spacing, as two rows of buttons. These buttons can relate to other features, such as the points of a collar or pocket placement, to create a larger visual grouping. If rows of buttons in the upper torso were grouped with a center front pleat in the lower torso the viewer's eye could move continuously, vertically up the center front of the body.

On the other hand, units may appear to segregate into visual parts. An example is seen in a black suit with a white shirt and red tie. The light-dark value contrast, the visual separation of the red tie surrounded by the white background, creates a strong visual pull to the upper torso. Value contrast provides a focal area. This contrast could create a visual separation from the rest of the body and clothing, which is not as contrasting.

The ABC and its inferred relations

Not all the relationships that influence the ABC are directly perceptible. Some are inferred associations and depend upon the viewer's past experiences

and expectations. As viewers we have many expectations, those of body appearance, coordinating colors, and appropriateness of ABC to event. These expectations are based upon our past experiences and cultural conditioning. What we attend to is often related to these expectancies—their predictability or our surprise when they are not met.

Certain expectations of event accompany the observation of an ABC within a given culture. Understanding the relationship requires knowing something about the event or circumstance of the ABC and specific social expectations accompanying the event. An expectation could be one of festivity and frivolity in one instance and of no-nonsense seriousness in another. If expectations are met by the association of the event with the ABC, the form may receive less attention from the viewer than if the ABC appears out of the expected circumstance. For example, viewing a swimming suit ABC on a beach is quite a different experience from viewing one in an office.

Priority in viewing— all things considered

The visual relations outlined above all potentially can attract our attention to the ABC, and which does so first is dependent upon the particular form and situation. For example, the viewer may be attracted first by the silhouette as a frame and subsequently notice the parts within the form. But often a visual part will attract attention first. For example, the head may attract first because of a distinct color difference at the head and neck from the rest of the ABC. The priority of the various attributes of the form are important to understand. But how they interrelate within the whole form is also important for the viewer to understand.

3

Observing the space of the ABC

THE goal in this chapter is to introduce a vocabulary that will aid the process of observing the space of the ABC. Awareness of how space is used is important in viewing the ABC as a whole. How space is viewed by the observer is dependent upon two types of orientation—the visual world and the visual field.

Two viewing orientations

To consider the perception of space we need to think about how we see, but not in the sense of the obvious—eyes open and focusing and sufficient light. We will assume these primary factors. Now we are considering two significant ways to perceive the ABC.

THE VISUAL WORLD. James J. Gibson in *Perception of the Visual World* described the visual world as that familiar space in which we ordinarily operate—an unbounded and extended environment filled with solid objects. We focus on these solid objects for meaning and action.

This visual world remains the same when the viewer moves. It is a surround of 360 degrees, extending beyond what can be immediately seen to what we know exists. It is the world perceived under ordinary circumstances by scanning and is based upon our past experiences and our memory for connecting those experiences with the present. Constancy of an object's attributes is a fact of the visual world—a book viewed from across the room is the same size as when the viewer is close by. If asked to describe a plate, a viewer whose perspective is the visual world describes only its roundness.

When attending to the visual world, the viewer sees space as having no center and no periphery. All things are clear, detailed, and stable. The viewer focuses on the objects in the space and does not attend to the spaces between them.

THE VISUAL FIELD. The visual field is less familiar to many viewers than the visual world because it is only observable through special effort. The visual field is perceived by fixing the eye at one point, then examining what can be viewed from that one point without attending to the point itself.

From a fixed position, consider what you can see out to your visual periphery without moving your head or eye. Try closing one eye to remove the effects of binocular vision. When one eye is closed, your nose appears at the periphery of this oval-shaped field. The visual field is approximately 180 degrees horizontally and 150 degrees vertically.

If you persist, the scene will resemble an oval-shaped picture with areas of colored, flattened surfaces divided by edges and contours. This scene has boundaries and therefore differs from the visual world. The field or "picture" should appear clear and sharp at the center and less clear at the edge.

In the visual field one object can eclipse another when it is in front of the other. When describing a plate, a viewer whose perspective is the visual field would describe the plate shape and size as changing relative to viewer position, one time appearing elliptical and small, another time round and large.

A comparison of the conditions of observation of the visual world and visual field indicates differences in perceiving shape and size. In the visual world objects remain a constant size and shape, whatever their distance or position. Surfaces of the three-dimensional form in the visual world remain constant from any viewing location (fig. 3.1).

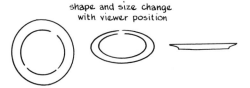

VISUAL FIELD – viewed from fixed position

shape and size change
with viewer position

VISUAL WORLD

objects remain constant
whatever distance or reference

3.1. Two viewer orientations are visual world and visual field. *James J. Gibson.* Perception of the Visual World, *p. 28. Copyright 1950, renewed 1978 by Houghton Mifflin Company. Used by permission.*

In the visual field, objects are not constant. They are smaller at a distance. Shape is defined by the outlines of the object viewed as projected on a plane. As expected, this planar shape changes with a change in viewing position. Even though the surfaces are not totally flat, they approximate depthlessness and take on a pictorial quality of flatness or two-dimensionality.

Thus viewing the ABC from the reference of the visual world or from that of the visual field makes a difference in what you see. The two approaches to viewing spaces need to be understood. Visual experience needs to be separated into what is seen in an unbounded visual world experience and what is seen in a bounded and defined visual field.

Priorities in viewing the ABC

When observing the ABC in its entirety, the viewer considers the space occupied by the ABC and how the adjacent area affects silhouette. The viewer must also consider the space between form and self, that is, foreground, or figure, and background space (fig. 3.2). If we

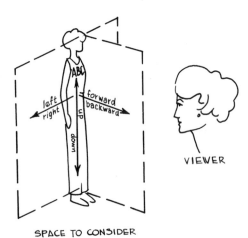

SPACE TO CONSIDER

3.2. The space of the ABC in a visual field includes left-right, up-down, and forward-backward.

are conscious of the way we view the ABC, we will soon become aware of the visual priority of certain attributes—the difference in their ability to attract focus. The following vocabulary is intended to aid the observer in becoming aware of the priorities in the way the ABC occupies space and in categorizing that space.

CLOSED OR OPEN. How the silhouette defines the form is a factor in how it occupies space and attracts our attention. The silhouette can appear very distinct and independent of the surround or indistinct and interdependent with the surround. *Closed* or *open* are expressions of difference in the relation of the ABC to the surrounding space. These differences alter the visual effect of the ABC.

A closed form is self-contained, with the silhouette acting as a boundary. This effect of boundary is often a controlling factor in perception. When one views a closed form, the silhouette of the ABC appears isolated from surrounding space with a terminal edge (fig. 3.3). This is often caused by a contrast in value between form and space or by a continuous silhouette edge. Also convex shapes appear to enclose more than do concave, and often the closed form is mostly convex line. Visual movement of the viewer in taking in the ABC is contained within the envelope of the silhouette. The viewer does not feel any need to consider the space around the form because the form appears quite separate and distinct from it. A closed ABC is more immediately taken in by the viewer and is much simpler to perceive because of its clarity. Thus a closed ABC appears nearer to the observer.

In an open form the ABC and the surround appear to interact. An open form does not appear self-contained (fig. 3.4). The form and the surround are interde-

a   b   c

3.3. ABCs can appear closed to the adjacent surround. **a.** *Photo courtesy of University of Minnesota; designed by Sandra Thoreson.* **b.** *Photo courtesy of Bill Blass, Ltd.* **c.** *Photo courtesy of Division of Costume, The National Museum of American History, Smithsonian Institution.*

pendent. The outline of the ABC does not enclose as a boundary or edge but can appear to belong to one side as much as to the other. This can occur because the edge is not distinct and clear, as when the silhouette has transparent edges or is the same color as the surround. The silhouette may also appear open because it has many discontinuous lines that seem to incorporate the space around it. The silhouette often does not direct the viewer to essential informa-

3.4. ABCs can appear open to the adjacent surround. **a.** *Photo courtesy of University of Minnesota; Adrian Retrospective.* **b.** *Photo courtesy of Minneapolis College of Art and Design; designed by Catherine Steinfest Eisler.* **c.** *Photo courtesy of Minneapolis College of Art and Design; designed by Theresa Trone.*

a   b   c

tion. Instead the visual movement may be directed to the central axis of the ABC, for example, or to the surface. The silhouette is not a dominant force in viewing the ABC. On the contrary, it may be ambiguous or even seem to disappear. The open form seems more distant from the observer.

When the ABC is moving, the viewer is attracted to the movement. The ABC in motion has different capabilities for interaction with the surround and can appear open because of the floating effect of a lightweight fabric. A closed form that is moving may become more open because the materials trail the ABC. For example, a two-piece business suit contrasting with the surround would ordinarily appear closed. But in motion this suit, especially with the jacket unbuttoned, may trail the wearer and thus appear to interact more with the surround.

Closed and open are at either end of a continuum of visual effects created by the differences in how the observer views the relation of the ABC to the surround. At the extreme of open, the actual boundary of the silhouette may be difficult to distinguish. It may be blurred or disappearing as it interacts with the surround. In between closed and open range other examples, such as an ABC with a direct and simple silhouette but also with a striped surface that interferes with the continuity of the silhouette and becomes a viewing priority. The continuum of closed and open visual effects will be expanded by each viewer with the experience of perceiving a wide range of ABCs with this factor in mind. Think of the most extreme example of an open and closed ABC and then fill in the continuum with ABCs that fall between the two. The continuum looks like this:

Closed	Open
Distinct convex edge	Vague concave edge
Continuous simple line	Discontinuous complex line

WHOLE OR PART. A visual part is a unit of the whole that has a measure of separation or distinction from the rest of the ABC. It can be as small as one button and as large as the upper torso of the body or the entire silhouette. What initially separates for viewing may be the whole form or one or more smaller parts. The question in categorizing a form according to *whole* or *part* is what separates first for viewing.

Organizing means perceiving or taking in the ABC by some visual path. Generally the ABC is designed to involve the viewer in some degree of order or sequencing of parts as they relate to the whole or vice versa. The ABC and the relation of its details can make a difference in what is viewed first—whether the whole or part stands out in perception.

Whole-to-part viewing occurs when the observer views the whole first and then the parts. This process occurs as the observer scans the entire ABC, consciously taking in its entirety. However, the process of viewing depends not only on the viewer but also on the form. Instances when the form is likely to be viewed first as a whole are numerous. If the silhouette is distinct, creating a boundary for the ABC, the whole is likely to be viewed first. When the ABC is all matte black and the surface does not subdivide into parts within the silhouette, the whole will be viewed first. When the surface is covered overall with a small, distinct repeated shape and the silhouette is the most important continuous shape of the ABC, the whole will be viewed first (fig. 3.5).

The ABC will also be viewed first in its entirety when parts are interdependent. An example of this type of whole-to-part viewing occurs when an ABC has a number of visual parts that have soft edges because of a textural but not a noticeable color difference. Carol Chan-

3.5. These ABCs will be viewed first as a whole. **a.** *Designed by Bonnie Cashin. Used by permission.* **b.** *Photo courtesy of University of Minnesota; designed by Amy Gerlinger.* **c.** *Photo courtesy of Minneapolis' College of Art and Design; designed by Pamela Tyree Kirton.*

ning has said she likes to look "all of a piece." She accomplishes this by dressing in a white matte surface overall and because her hair and skin are light in value. She has created soft edges within the silhouette and she often appears as a whole first.

Part-to-whole viewing takes place when the observer views the parts first and then the whole (fig. 3.6). Part-to-whole viewing is largely due to relatively independent parts in an ABC, i.e., clear edge definition of shapes or contrast of surface that overrides the effect of the

3.6. These ABCs will be viewed first as parts. **a.** *Photo courtesy of Andrew Fezza Menswear; photographer, Thom Gilbert.* **b.** *Photo courtesy of University of Minnesota, designed by Lana Sultze.* **c.** *Photo courtesy of Chou Chou, St. Paul, Minnesota.*

silhouette as a whole. The use of the term *separates* refers to the visual effect of viewing parts first and then the whole.

Body coloring can create visual parts. For example, when Carol Channing wears black, her head (both skin and hair) become a visual part. The same part effect could be created with dark hair and a light-value surface near the neck.

The part-to-whole relation can be considered on a continuum. Those ABCs that are viewed as parts first usually have several distinct parts that direct the observer. But there are other combinations of part-to-whole relations; for example, the form may have only one distinct visual part as a focus. This often happens with the business suit where an area near the face is contrasting in value and/or hue, pattern, or texture. The remainder of the body, which fits one's expectancy of "suitness," is only scanned. Some details that are expected may go unnoticed.

The continuum of what is viewed first with reference to the part looks like this:

Part		Whole
Distinct parts	One distinct part	Indistinct parts

PLANAR SEPARATION OR INTEGRATION. The term *figure-ground* is a way to express the spatial relationships of the parts to the whole ABC. The silhouette is the frame of reference of the visual field and the plane from which the ABC projects toward the viewer. Thus, the space between the viewer and the form enters the awareness of the viewer and is expressed as the planar relation of figure to ground.

The definition of *figure* is that which has object quality or "thingness" in our viewing. It is what we focus upon. Ground provides a frame of reference for figure and appears to surround and lie beneath it. Figure generally appears to exist somewhere in front of ground.

How far figure lies in front of ground determines whether it distinctly separates from ground or integrates with it.

The relation of figure to ground changes as the viewer focuses on different areas of the ABC. In figure 3.7, when the viewer focuses on the pocket, the star advances as figure because it is surrounded by the lighter value of the pocket. However, when the entire shape of the bib is considered, the pocket can become figure. Then the star can appear almost as a hole in the pocket because of the similar value of the star and bib.

3.7. A figure-ground relation in an apparel item can change depending upon viewer focus. *Photo courtesy of University of Minnesota; photographer, Leo Perry.*

Figure can relate to ground at different levels of apparent closeness for the viewer (fig 3.8). Figure can appear to lie on a plane very close to the plane of the ground, to be relatively integrated

a   b   c

3.8. Planar integration in the ABC **(a)** grades to planar separation **(c)**. **a.**
Photo courtesy of Oscar de la Renta, Ltd.; photo by Jesse Gerstein. **b.**
Photo courtesy of Dimitri Couture, Ltd., New York, Milano. **c.** *Photo
courtesy of Bill Blass, Ltd.*

with the ground. This can occur with closely graded values or intensities or with similar sizes of shapes. Figure as small shapes on a surface can appear to lie quite close to the ground when in a value close to the ground, e.g., small navy blue polka dots or stripes on a black ground.

Figure can also appear relatively separated from ground. The plane where the figure lies can appear at a considerable distance from the plane of the ground, as in the case of a medium-sized navy blue polka dot on an opaque white ground. In a pattern of shapes on a surface, this sometimes has been called a spotty effect because it presents to the viewer a complete segregation of figure from ground. The viewer attraction value of each shape is high.

Figure has also been referred to as positive shape, or focal viewing, and ground as negative space, or contextual viewing. The observer usually picks out positive shapes or surfaces for focus because they are what make the most sense or carry the most meaning. It is more difficult to be aware of the place of ground

in viewing; it requires the perspective of the visual field.

We need to maintain an awareness of what is figure and what is ground. There are certain features of the ABC that tend to be viewed as figure, such as simple shapes that appear to enclose and separate from the adjacent space. Every time the viewer distinguishes or separates an entire object or one of its visual parts from the background, the planar relation is influencing perspective.

In applying the planar concept, the viewer is not concerned with what is actually on top but with which surface appears to advance. For example, the viewer knows a jacket worn open is on top of the accompanying shirt. But the shirt may very well be functioning as figure and the jacket as ground. The shirt, in such an instance, could be a more intense, warm color than the jacket.

When the ABC is viewed, the body or clothes may vary in their visual priority because of what is perceived as figure. For example, the body in a bathing suit may provide more awareness of the body than of the clothing as figure, but not always. Amount of body covered, degree of curvature of shape, or value contrast are factors in whether the body or the clothing is viewed first. Either the clothing or the body can provide the figure or focus in the figure-ground relation. To become aware of exactly what is figure is valuable in understanding whether a neckline belongs more as figure to the neck or to the apparel (fig. 3.9).

Reversals in figure-ground or positive-negative space occur either because of the character of the ABC and the surround or because the viewer forces re-

3.10. The viewer first groups the light parts as figure on dark ground. At another time the black surface can be perceived as figure. *Photo courtesy of Bill Blass, Ltd.; photographer, Gideon Lewin.*

3.9. Body parts can become figure. *Photo courtesy of University of Minnesota; designed by Vicki Johnson.*

versals in his experience of the figure-ground relation (fig. 3.10). In other words, the active viewer may switch what is first seen as figure to ground during the scanning process. This is a useful skill to foster. For example, initially we may focus on the entire ABC as figure and the space around as ground. Then, we may focus on one part that attracts our attention, as figure. The surrounding area becomes ground. Often the viewer can force reversals even though the figure-ground relation is relatively clear. This practice of making reversals can help in a better understanding of the relationship. Both figure and ground are important to the visual effect of the ABC. But since noting planar relationships is not ordinarily necessary in carrying on life events, the viewer needs to make conscious what is figure and ground.

Figure-ground ambiguity is the term used when this relationship can easily be reversed or switched by the viewer. This can occur because the cues for "figuredness" are not clear or because as the viewer focuses on various parts of the ABC, there is no clear dominance of one or the other. This reversal may be stimulating or somewhat disturbing, depending upon the flexibility of the viewer. We have all experienced the reversal of meaning in two-dimensional examples of the face or goblet reversal (fig. 3.11). In the ABC the reversal may or may not change the meaning. But often cues for figuredness are introduced in the design of an ABC to make clear the figure-ground relation.

The continuum of planar separation to integration looks like this:

Planar Separation	Planar Integration
Distinct edge	Indistinct edges
Discrete shapes dispersed on surface	Interrelated shapes filling surface

FLAT OR ROUNDED. How surfaces occupy space needs to be differentiated by the viewer. From the perspective of the visual world, we know the ABC is a three-dimensional form in space. However, we may perceive its surfaces as three-dimensional, or rounded, or essentially as two-dimensional, flat surfaces, depending upon their nature (fig. 3.12).

At any one time the observer views only one side of an ABC. The viewer who takes note of silhouette—the outermost perimeter of the ABC that can be viewed from one side—is viewing a two-dimensional or planar aspect. The viewer who takes note of how a shiny-surfaced fabric interacts with body curvature is viewing a three-dimensional or cylindrical aspect of the ABC. The ABC can give three-dimensional cues, which direct viewing of the ·ABC as a cylinder with a surface. This depends on the manner in which the body is treated by the surfaces and shapes of the garment and

a

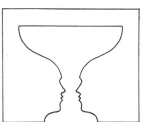

b

3.11. Figure-ground ambiguity can create reversals depending upon viewer focus. **a.** *Photo courtesy of University of Minnesota; photographer, Michelle Madson.* **b.** *Photo courtesy of Minneapolis College of Art and Design; designed by Sharon Wendel.*

a   b

3.12. Surfaces of the ABC can appear rounded or flat. **a.** *Photo courtesy of Polyester Fashion Council.* **b.** *Photo courtesy of Kleibacker historic costume collection; 1920s silk panne velvet.*

the configurations that can be applied to a conforming material such as fabric, e.g., easing, gathering, pleating.

The surfaces of the ABC will always influence what the viewer will perceive. For example, some surfaces that do not reflect off of the body curvatures will appear more two-dimensional, flat, and essentially on a plane parallel to the viewer. These surfaces can be viewed as essentially flat even though the viewer knows the body is a cylindrical surface with many curves. The surfaces of the garment can hang straight down from the shoulders because of gravity and not interact with the body curves. When a surface appears to be relatively unoccupied, without texture or light reflectance, the focus is on shape. Then the eye perceives the area as a block of color, and edge can become a priority. This can occur in a matte black that does not call attention to surface contours but to area and silhouette.

The apparel can also appear to em-phasize the rounded contours and curves of the body. Surfaces are often viewed as extending around the body simply because the viewer knows they do. But the viewer can also be made conscious of the rounded body shape through its interaction with fabric surfaces. This can be accomplished in various ways. Fabrics can be wrapped around the body to emphasize contour, such as with a sari or sarong. A diagonal ruffle encircling the body can emphasize the three-dimensional nature of the body. Attention can be called to the rounded surfaces of the body cylinder by a shiny fabric reflecting at different angles or by a printed surface that is distorted from regularity by the cylindrical nature of the body. But the print must be subtle and regular enough so that it does not demand to be viewed first. Surfaces can also appear rounded because of layout structuring, gathers or pleats. This will occur especially with medium-value surfaces because light and shadow effects can be carried by them.

The continuum of flat surfaces to rounded ones looks like this:

Flat	Rounded
Smooth, nonreflecting surfaces	Curved, reflecting surfaces
Planar shapes	Three-dimensional shapes

DETERMINATE OR INDETERMINATE. Determinate or indeterminate refers to the apparent thickness of the surfaces of the ABC and their distance from the observer. Reference is to the immediacy of the surfaces of the ABC for the viewer, that is, how near or far away they appear and how easily they are assimilated by the viewer (fig. 3.13).

Determinate describes surfaces that appear definite, sharp, regular, and clear cut. If shapes are present, they are few and simple or overall repetitious. The shapes are easily perceived as figure, while at the same time the viewer clearly perceives ground. The surface has relatively few planes or levels in viewing. There is no doubt about what is figure and what is ground. A determinate surface usually has little visual texture and carries little potential for light and shadow. The observer takes in the determinate surface quickly because of the immediacy in the way it occupies space.

An indeterminate surface appears less definite in the way it occupies space. The indeterminate surface often appears blurred or soft or with infinite levels or ambiguity of figure-ground. Shapes are irregular and soft edged. The surface appears thick because of overall visual texture. An example of an indeterminate surface would be a transparent surface with an ambiguous figure-ground relation. This would occur when the transparency was not backed with an opaque surface. Another example would be a reflecting surface that creates a myriad of

a   b

3.13. Surfaces of the ABC may be indeterminate or determinate. **a.** *Photo courtesy of Jhane Barnes; photographer, Jade Albert.* **b.** *Photo courtesy of Polyester Fashion Council.*

3.14. The polar terms describing the space of the ABC are applied to ABCs differing in visual effect. **a.** *Photo courtesy of Albert Nipon, fall 1984.* **b.** *Photo courtesy of Albert Nipon Collectibles, fall 1984.* **c.** *Photo courtesy of Minneapolis College of Art and Design; designed by Donneen Torrey.* **d.** *Photo courtesy of Minneapolis College of Art and Design; designed by Liz Rath Parr.*

different, interrelated light and shadow surface effects (fig. 3.12b). Gathers or pleats in a medium value that carry light and shadow effects could also appear indeterminate.

The continuum of surfaces defined by determinate to indeterminate looks like this:

Determinate	Indeterminate
Plain, smooth surface	Much surface texture
Few but regular or no shapes	Many irregular shapes
No light and shadow effect	Much light and shadow

Using the vocabulary of the ABC

The vocabulary describing the space of the ABC consists of five sets of polar word pairs, each representing, first of all, an extreme visual effect. In other words, the viewer learns about the forms of ABCs by locating the extreme forms at the ends of a continuum that can represent a range of degrees of a spatial phenomenon. ABCs can be compared using this vocabulary. Examples can be found to be placed all along the continuum. Furthermore, all five sets of word pairs can be applied to each ABC (fig. 3.14).

In addition, the word pairs interrelate when applied to ABCs. As the viewer categorizes ABCs according to each set of word pairs, certain combinations will often reoccur together. For example, closed and determinate are often connected in the same ABC. As the individual terminology becomes understood, and each of the word pairs is applied to repeated ABCs, over time a certain relatedness between the concepts will be found. But, do they always link together in the same way? No, they do not. An ABC can be closed and indeterminate. Look for one.

Visual exercises

I. Analysis of the ABC: Begin with a frame.
   A. Select two ABCs with very different silhouettes. Using a blank sheet of tracing paper, trace the entire silhouette of each ABC.
   B. Concentrating on the entire silhouette, explain the relation of the body silhouette to the ABC silhouette. What influence can silhouette have on viewing the total ABC? What factors of the surrounding space can influence the viewing of the silhouette?

II. Understanding polar word pairs referring to uses of space in the ABC.
   A. Select at least four ABCs that can be placed on the continuums represented by the following five word pairs: open-closed, part-whole, planar integration-separation, flat-rounded, determinate-indeterminate.
   B. Describe the differences in visual effect among the selected ABCs using the five word pairs.

4

The body as a preexisting structure

EVERYONE'S body is individual. A person would not be recognized without his or her unique qualities. We use many terms to describe the human body—*male, tall, child, large.* Further, in our usual view of the body, we are interacting with a structure more or less similar to ourselves and this influences what we see. We compare what we see to ourselves and to others; for example, we view a form as shorter or taller than ourselves.

The goal of this chapter is to become more aware of what we already know about viewing the body. We are so intimately acquainted with the body—our own and others—that we do not stop to think about what it offers visually. We constantly interact with other people who influence our actions. We become experts at recognizing another person with a minimum of visual cues. Yet we are sensitive to variation in visual effect; we are quick to notice changes in someone's appearance, even though we do not know exactly what the change is.

For purposes of visual analysis, we want to alter our visual habit of using a minimum number of cues to accomplish recognition. We will separate ourselves from the familiar body and reaffirm the specific attributes that make it up. The body will be discussed as a generalized visual structure and then its various features delineated.

The body, considered as a basic vis-

ual structure, has many universal aspects. How can we describe the human body as to its form qualities? What about its structure is common? As the observer viewing the body, for a time we will separate from viewing the qualities that make the body individual. To concentrate on the body as a generalized form will help us relate the body structure to the materials arranged upon it. The potential influence of the body structure upon organization of the ABC will be better understood.

First, the body will be described as a physical structure that already exists. Then the body as a component of the ABC will be considered. Finally, the body will be considered as it suggests associations that affect our viewing of the ABC.

The body as a physical structure

The body consists of a trunk, head, and four limbs, or extremities. The body exists naturally in a hierarchical relationship; it is a vertical unit, generally considered to have more visual interest at the top. The head is usually predominant in our viewing of the body. It offers the most visual detail and its size, rounded shape, and position, centered on top of the body, make it a natural focal point. Also, the contrast of the head shape with shoulder width increases the importance of this area as a center of attention.

Head length is the unit of visual measure for the body and its proportions; thus the body is described as a certain number of heads high. The head

tened oval or elliptical cylinder (fig. 4.3). A cross section of any body segment would vary in circumference depending upon where the cross section was taken. The body limbs are also cylindrical but

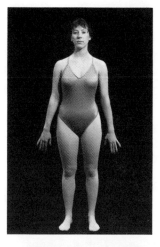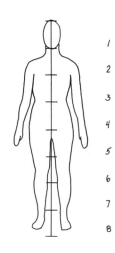

4.1. Head length of an adult female used as a proportional measure. *Photo courtesy of University of Minnesota; Trish Stoik, model.*

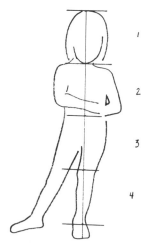

4.2. Head length of a child used as a proportional measure. *Photo courtesy of University of Minnesota; Laura Hollihan, model.*

length of a particular body is used for measuring that body (figs. 4.1, 4.2). A smaller or a larger head on the same size body can make quite a difference in proportion and overall appearance.

The body torso is a convex cylindrical surface. A cross section viewed from the top down would appear as a flat-

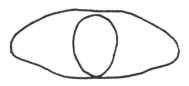

4.3. The body cylinder viewed from the top down.

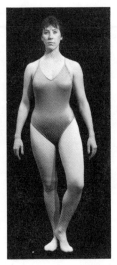

4.4. The female and male bodies viewed from the front or back and side. *Photos courtesy of University of Minnesota; James Wolfe and Trish Stoik, models.*

smaller in size than the torso. The curve of the cylinder affects the appearance of a surface placed upon it. A body cylinder has a flatter curve when viewed from the front or back and a fuller curve when viewed from the side (fig. 4.4).

The body is a vertical gradation of size and detail. The arms are similar to the legs, only shorter in length and smaller in circumference. The upper portion of the body contains more visual detail than the lower portion. As the body is viewed from the front or back, the arms and legs are in symmetrical pairs. Context of body parts in relation to each other affects how we view the ABC. The body, whether tall or short, wide or narrow, can affect the contextual association of body parts.

The body structure is a symmetrical form about a vertical axis when viewed from the front or back. The body has several points along the vertical axis where width appears greatest (fig. 4.5). As one views the body structure, this wide point helps to frame the ABC. From the front the shoulder width contrasts with the head width. Thus the shoulders can be an important point of emphasis. A second wide point is the area where the wrists and lower hip meet when the body is still and the arms are hanging in a relaxed position.

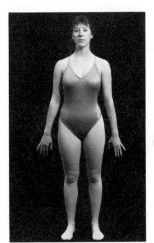

4.5. The body can be viewed from the front as having a vertical axis, with a horizontal line at width of shoulder and hips. *Photo courtesy of University of Minnesota.*

The widest point can change, as, for example, when the legs are spread and the body appears grounded by the wide point being near the ground. Hands resting in position on the high hip with arms bent can raise the wide part of the body structure. When the arms are raised to a horizontal position, the wide point of the body again changes and the torso by contrast appears narrower.

When the body is viewed from the side it is asymmetrical (fig. 4.6). An im-portant aspect of the body is that it moves about and changes position. When the arms are swinging they can create a diversion for the observer. The arms in a hugging position increase the emphasis on the body cylinder. The body can create another kind of visual effect when bent over at the waist. Think of other variations the body can present by moving about and changing position (fig. 4.7).

Body locomotion can vary greatly in

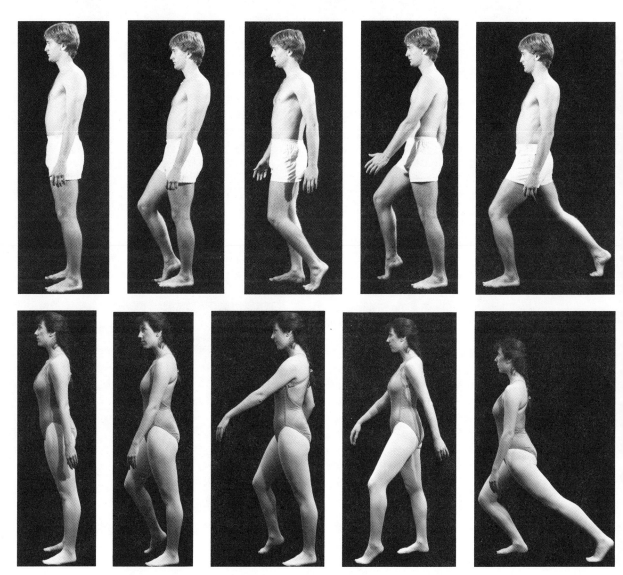

4.6. The body from the side view is asymmetric. *Photos courtesy of University of Minnesota; photographer, Leo Perry.*

4.7. The body moves about and changes positions. *Photos courtesy of University of Minnesota.*

direction, speed, and economy of movement. Large, slow sweeping motions and small, quick jerky motions can occur with little warning of the change for the viewer. Forward movement is most common but the body can move in all directions. The direction of most-limited movement is up and down. The body's potential for movement has to do with gravitational effects on the body.

The body's relation to gravity is also important to its overall visual effect. The torso and limbs relate to gravity and maintenance of body balance, especially when the body moves. The body usually appears to be in dynamic equilibrium and when it is not, the viewer often feels tension in his own body. Most of the time the body appears to be grounded. The trunk and upper limbs can be adjusted; the lower limbs can be spread to gain and maintain balance.

BODY VIEWS. An observer of the body knows of its structure but may not have thought about its visual effect in terms of body views. We take for granted what we see frequently and the way we see it from our visual world perspective (discussed in chap. 3). However, what

 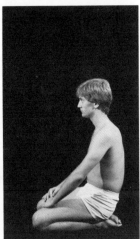

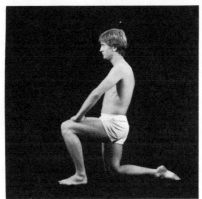

can be viewed at any one time depends upon the relation of the observer to a particular body structure, to the visual field. The extent of the body that can be viewed at any one time influences its units for design.

A visual field, as you will remember, is that portion of the visual world that can be perceived by an observer from a fixed position. The visual field of an observer is normally composed of a variety of objects. To perceive the form of any one of these objects requires an observer first to segregate the object from the rest of the visual field and then to observe its details. This segregation process requires an observer to concentrate on one object

4 / The body as a preexisting structure **41**

at a time in the visual field.

From the frame of reference of a visual field, the body has visual units or views, front, back, and side views. The front view is the visual unit of the body that receives the most attention. This is perhaps due to the position and the details of the head, the body symmetry, and the way the body moves. We interact as one human to another mostly from the front view and this often affects how the ABC is designed to be viewed. However, examples of ABCs can be found that emphasize other body views.

From the standpoint of the visual field, the body structure can present two general form characteristics—planar and depth shape. When the body is viewed as having a silhouette, the observer is perceiving a planar, or flat shape. This silhouette is the farthest shape from the observer and is an outline that characterizes one body view (fig. 4.1). This silhouette shape achieves a framing for the ABC. The actual body contour may be obscured, as when a long jacket skims over the waist ignoring the contour between full chest and hip. The body outline can be extended with shapes of clothing to emphasize the horizontal or vertical axis (fig. 4.8). The silhouette of the body can close off the surrounding space and thus attract viewer attention to the shape. In the

depth or three-dimensional shape the body is viewed as consisting of varying rounded surfaces that protrude from the silhouette, extending toward the viewer.

The appearance of planar and depth shapes of the body can be affected by their treatment as surfaces. If the silhouette is emphasized, the form may appear closed and flat; if deemphasized, the form appears more open. If the depth shape is emphasized, the form appears three-dimensional and rounded (refer to chap. 3 for discussion).

The body as potential for the ABC

The ABC is a variation and an interpretation of the body structure (fig. 4.9). The relation between the body and what is arranged upon it depends upon whether the arrangement is a relation of similarity or difference. In one instance the body may be evident in its contours because a material is stretched over the body surface, as is a leotard. But while the contours become more evident, the body textures, such as body hair and kneecap, are covered over and minimized. The vertical axis of the body may be repeated by a center line of a jacket and contrasted by the horizontal width of a large sleeve. Thus surfaces can mimic the body curvatures and at the

a

b

4.8.
Apparel may extend body shape horizontally and vertically. **a.** *Designed by Yvonne Karlsson. Used by permission.* **b.** *Photo courtesy of Fairchild Visuals, division of Fairchild Publications, Inc., New York City.*

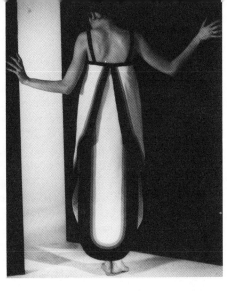

4.9.
Front and back body views illustrate variations of the body structure. *Photo courtesy of Minneapolis College of Art and Design; designed by Liz Rath Parr.*

same time cover the body textures.

The ABC can emphasize one part of the body, at the same time minimizing or ignoring another. A body segment,. such as head, legs, hips, or trunk, can be emphasized. Often this is accomplished by contrasting one portion of the body with a shape placed upon it. A big shirt could contrast with a narrower treatment of the hip area, or color values could contrast a black sweater with light-value skin and hair. Contrast of a body feature with other shapes can emphasize the difference and thus modify the appearance of the body segment.

The entire body structure may be emphasized in various ways. The ABC may change the relations of the body structure by combining body segments (fig. 4.8a). The legs and the trunk of the body, for example, combine in a floor-length skirt and extend the shape of the trunk vertically. A cape combining the limbs and torso can extend the visual effect of the trunk horizontally (fig. 4.10). Surfaces can skim the body silhouette and thus modify its visual effect (fig. 4.8b). They can repeat the body shape or color and emphasize the whole.

The arrangement of materials on the body can increase the perception of the body as a series of units—front, back, and several sides. It matters which unit

we are viewing. From the front or back we see bilateral symmetry while a side view is bilaterally asymmetric. A designer can treat the front of the body as the most important unit for viewing. A

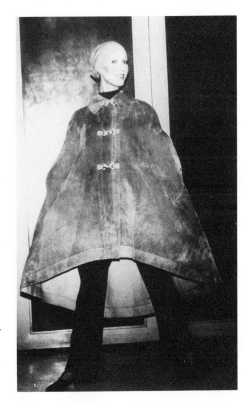

4.10. A cape can help to combine body segments. *Designed by Bonnie Cashin. Used by permission.*

4 / The body as a preexisting structure **43**

man's suit is a typical front-view treatment with the center front lapels, tie, and belt buckle as points of focus. Viewing the trouser legs, either the silhouette or the space between the legs, as a continuation of this front treatment can create a vertical eye movement for the observer.

Surfaces of the ABC can be structured so the body surfaces are viewed as flattened. Use of a matte black surface is one way to make the body appear to have a flattened surface. Even though the material may follow the rounded surfaces closely, to the viewer the body appears flattened like a paper doll, with the shape of the silhouette as a strong visual attraction.

The ABC can also lead us to view the body as a rounded surface. The treatment of the body surfaces can enhance the rounded effect of the body. For example, a line continuing around the body, diagonal stripes that are not too dominant, or a reflecting surface smoothly contouring the body calls our attention to the rounded contours. The viewing unit may not even appear to be complete from only one side of the body. An observer may feel a strong urge to follow around the body to satisfy curiosity and discover how a line is continued (fig. 4.11).

The body is basically vertical, longer than it is wide, with but few exceptions. This verticality is often repeated with the form of the ABC and is emphasized in long, close-to-the-body caftans, trousers, and skirts. Treatment of the body silhouette as a triangular shape, a gradation from wider at the bottom narrowing to the head, is also a way to emphasize body verticality. The observer is directed to the gradual narrowing in viewing the ABC.

The body trunk is a convex cylindrical surface, which is elliptical when viewed from the top down. The relatively flat center front area is often used for a focus to repeat and therefore emphasize the verticality of the body. A panel of buttons or pleats or even a collar coming together at center front are examples of use of this flattened area for visual detail and focus.

The body limbs are more truly cylindrical than the trunk, and thus the curve is more highly graded. Often this graded curve of the limbs is utilized in the ABC. Pants often emphasize the continuous rounded surface. Small, closely graded checks provide for visual attention to the rounded cylinder. Seams or ruffles spiraled around the arms or legs are another way for a designer to call atten-

4.11.
The lines created by fabric folds continue around the ABC. *Photo courtesy of University of Minnesota; designed by Georgia Scheu.*

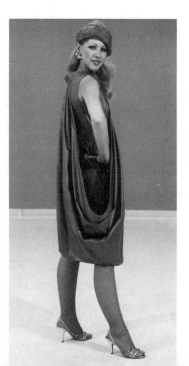

tion to the cylindrical nature of the body.

The limbs can create more space for the ABC by extending the horizontal or vertical axis, depending upon how they are positioned. Designers sometimes utilize this body characteristic by having models extend their arms horizontally to increase the visual space of the ABC. Religious vestments are often designed to extend visual space, incorporating the space of the arms outstretched horizontally by a robe with wide sleeves.

BODY SURFACES. The surfaces of the body are visually textured. Skin has a texture that may appear relatively smooth to somewhat rough as in a freckled surface or the surface of the elbow joint or kneecap. Other body textures are those of the toenails and fingernails. Hair can range from smooth and straight to curly or kinky, from matte to shiny. Hair on the arms and legs appears different in texture, spacing, and length from head or facial hair and often serves a different visual function. Head and facial hair can create shapes because of their density and length, while body hair only provides surface interest.

Body colors include skin colors, hair colors, and eye colors. These colors can be very similar to each other or offer visual contrast in hue, value, and intensity. The relations of skin, hair, and eye color are an important part of the body context for an ABC. Consider the effects of similar values of dark brown skin and black hair or the effect of the contrast of cool blue-white skin and black hair. The latter offers value contrast and a natural focus for the viewer, while the former has potential for contrast with lighter surfaces placed upon the ABC.

Body hues of skin, hair, and eyes can range from being similar to opposite (or contrasting) in position on the color wheel. For example, a contrast in body hues may be yellow tones in hair, red tones in the skin, and blue eyes. Some contrasts in hue, value, and intensity are present in small areas of the body, e.g., the eye and lashes. Though skin covers the largest area, we are often least aware of its color because of its subtlety of hue.

Body colors may be maximized, minimized, or ignored by the ABC. Visual relationships contrasting the body colors with the surfaces worn on the body can be viewed in some ABCs, for example, light with dark value, cool with warm color. Relationships of similarity between body colors and surfaces worn on the body can also be viewed. When the relation is similar, the body colors do not become a focus. When the relation is different, even though subtle, the body colors can become focus, often with the head as figure and the remainder of the ABC as ground. An example of such a subtle difference would be use of a less intense but otherwise similar color in clothing to hair. The hair would attract the viewer to the head as figure.

The body surfaces can be treated in various ways in the ABC. They can be revealed and smoothed with oils and creams or highlighted with color cosmetics. They can be covered and modified with a fabric surface that closely follows the body contour, such as a leotard or swimsuit. The surfaces of the body can thus interact with the surfaces placed upon the body.

BODY PARTS. The natural physical relation of body parts can be used in the ABC to provide a visual connection. For example, the position of shoulders to head is used for focus in collars and necklines. A turtleneck not only creates a longer line of the torso, it can also appear as a transition between the torso and head. The waist may be a focus when indented by a belt or be ignored with a jacket that skims the waist contour creating a transition between upper and lower torso. The

4.12. The body can appear grounded and balanced with lower limbs spread and arms extended. *Photo courtesy of University of Minnesota; designed by Mary Elleson-Jones.*

grounding can be aided or abetted in the design of the ABC. A figure skater or ballet dancer wears shoes to effect an airy, ungrounded appearance for the viewer. However, the heavy boots of a mountain climber or snow shoes ground the body not only visually but functionally.

Body parts can appear very much segregated as visual parts. The cape that at one time appears to visually unify the body torso and limbs also can make the head appear as a separate part. If the cape was a dark-value blue and the person wearing it had yellow hair and skin, the visual separation of the head would be distinct. On the other hand, a hood of the same color worn covering the head would unify the head with the torso and limbs, framing the face for visual focus (fig. 4.13).

position of the end of a sleeve affects the appearance of the trunk—the line of the sleeve can continue the bottom line of a jacket.

The head and face are usually dominant in our viewing of the body, often becoming a psychological priority. Examples abound where the head is used as an area for focus with the modification or treatment of materials placed upon it. The face may be framed by a hood or a cut of hair. Many details that attract are found there, such as brightly colored hats and earrings.

The body has implications for other visual effects, that is, it usually appears grounded and balanced (fig. 4.12). The longer lower limbs are often slightly spread to balance the body either standing still or in movement. The concept of

4.13. The face framed by materials creates visual focus. *Designed by Traci Scherek; photographer, Jonté. Used by permission.*

BODY MOVEMENTS. The body through movement has great potential for interaction with the materials placed upon it. The effect of gravity on body movement and on various weights of fabric can offer much visual variety and can attract viewer attention. Body movement can be affected, for example, by a crisp fabric that hangs from the shoulders, skimming the body surfaces. The effect achieved can be one of stately elegance because body movements often become restricted to slow sweeping motions. We somehow expect the body movements to follow those that we anticipate from the movements of the ABC (fig. 4.14).

On the other hand, imagine a buoyant lightweight fabric, such as chiffon, which moves with the body, resisting the immediate body contours but following the body with a slight lag (fig. 4.15). A body and fabric in motion can achieve a floating, butterfly effect. A silk scarf in a breeze can create a lilting, flowing movement away from the moving body, thus extending the space of the body.

The ABC is often designed with body movement in mind. For example, a wedding dress can extend backward as the bride moves down the aisle. A skating costume with a circular skirt takes advantage of the circular movements of the skater, creating a circle outward from the body.

Body movement is a considerable attraction for the viewer. In fact body movement is such a strong stimulus that it may be more stimulating than the ar-

4.14. Stiff materials used on the body often anticipate body movements. **a.** *Designed by Bonnie Cashin. Used by permission.* **b.** *Photo by Margot Siegel; designed by Ralph Lauren. Used by permission.*

a

b

4.15. A lightweight material moves with the body, resisting immediate body contours but following the body with a slight lag. *Photo courtesy of Minneapolis College of Art and Design; designed by June Getsug Banét.*

rangement of the materials upon the body. Thus body movements may play a large role in attracting attention to the ABC. An apparel designer expects varying degrees of movement from the wearer—walking, raising the arms, bending. However, body movements may be encumbered or restricted, as with a skirt that limits the stride.

An ABC that allows for uninhibited movement may involve a minimum of organization and instead may rely upon the natural arrangement of the body structure. The most uninhibiting material would be a substance that stretches over the body, such as in a leotard. Such a material allows a minimal obstruction of body movements. However, if the ultimate goal of all ABCs were to allow for the most body movement, the eventual solution might be no clothing at all.

MEANING ASSOCIATED WITH THE BODY. Certain parts of the body are associated with various processes and functions that affect the observer's viewing. How we view the ABC and associate meaning

may depend upon body emphasis. For example, focus on the head may be associated with intellect. Focus at the neckline, e.g., a shirt and tie contrasting with the rest of the body treatment, is recommended in no-nonsense dressing for business. The hands are often considered in their function of touching and feeling. Thus a focus on the hands with a sleeve ruffle may be associated with a feeling, caring person.

Sometimes the association depends upon the way the body is treated by such aspects as shaping and coloring. Body features often associated with youth are long, slender limbs and body curvatures minimized by the shapes placed upon the body. Colors are often light values or intense primary hues. Those associations that suggest maturity stress body curvatures, the use of a belt to change the shape of the figure and create visual focus. Colors that suggest maturity include dark values and muted secondary hues.

Expectations and past experiences of the viewer have an effect on body associations. For example, the blue jeans worn by so many and seen so often were eventually a standard item in our viewing, an equalizer of the lower torso. We no longer needed to notice them, until the details began to be worth noting, e.g., labels, stitching, color, fit.

BODY-CLOTHES PRIORITY. What visual relationships do we need to be aware of in order to understand how the body interacts in the ABC? How does the context of a particular body influence what is placed upon it? When, for example, does the body become ground for the figure of the clothing or the clothing become ground for the body as figure?

When one perceives the ABC, the body or clothes may vary in visual priority (i.e., amount of viewer focus) (fig. 4.16). At one extreme are clothes that are related directly to the display of the body curvatures. At the other extreme, the body may be used only as a hanger for garments, as with robes where the actual body curvatures are minimized. Shapes of the clothes can make the body appear to expand as a horizontal solid. The variation between a display of body and a display of clothes causes a difference in the general visual effect of the ABC. It is always important to consider the visual interrelations of body and

4.16. Body-clothes priority can change with various ABCs. **a.** *Photo courtesy of Minneapolis College of Art and Design; designed by Karen Heddens.* **b.** *Designed by Traci Scherek; photographer, Jonté. Used by permission.*

a

b

4.17. What is the body bringing to the ABC? *Photo courtesy of University of Minnesota; Laura Hollihan, model.*

clothing, that is, their dependence-independence. The clothing or the body can provide the primary viewing focus.

To understand specifically how the body is utilized in the ABC requires the viewer to analyze and compare the differences and similarities between the body as a preexisting structure and the visual form presented by the ABC. The ABC involves variations that occur because of the placement and emphasis of surfaces and the relation of these surfaces to body structure. The body has a preexisting structure that can be utilized differently in different ABCs. It is useful in viewing the ABC to ask, What is the body bringing to the organization? (fig. 4.17).

It is also important to be able to consider the body as a generalized structure in responding to the ABC, that is, the viewer who is engrossed with the ABC as a visual form becomes aware of the similarities of one human body to another and at the same time of the differences that create individuality. The

form of the ABC is always fascinating because it is human and we are attracted by its humanness. The analysis of the ABC is distinguished from the analysis of other visual forms because of the pervading sense of the human qualities present. But, on the other hand, by considering the body's visual similarities as a form, we can also understand its potential for variety in the ABC.

Visual exercises

I. Understanding body priority–clothing priority.
   A. Find two ABCs, one each to illustrate body priority and clothing priority.
   B. Explain how you view each and what about each illustrates the priority.

II. Understanding body views in the ABC.
   A. Find examples of ABCs that treat the body in the following ways: (1) one body view, front as a main visual unit; (2) one body view, back as a main visual unit; and (3) the body treated differently from multiple views.

B. Write a brief summary explaining how each ABC illustrates a different focus in body view.

III. Uses made of body focus by public figures.
   A. Persons who are seen frequently in public often have to consider their appearance as it affects their audience. Depending upon the nature of their job, they might have to consider whether the part or the whole is a focus and how an area of the body can become a focus. What different focus areas could be desirable for three different public figures (e.g., newscaster, dancer, politician)?
   B. Give some descriptive examples of different focuses you believe might be considered by each.

IV. Observing the ABC in motion.
   A. Observe an ABC still and in motion.
   B. What changes occur because of the body movements? Identify factors that may contribute to changes observed.

V. Understanding the physical factors of the body in the ABC.
   A.
      1. Select two persons for analysis with different hair, skin, and eye color.
      2. Obtain color chips from a paint store or other color source.
      3. Match color chips to colors found present in the skin, hair, and eyes of each person. Group the colors and label as to the body location.
      4. Compare the two groupings of color chips. Describe the colors. Refer to the *Munsell Book of Color, Neighboring Hues Edition,* to describe colors according to a notation system.
   B.
      1. Select two persons for analysis who vary in height. Ask them to wear clothing that is close to the body so as not to interfere with identification of body points.
      2. Measure head length of the two people. This can be done by having each one stand in front of a piece of paper of his or her height. A vertical line is marked alongside the person on the paper. Horizontal marks can be made on the paper as follows: Establish head length by marking the distance from the top of the head to the base of the chin. A square (an instrument having two sides that form a 90-degree angle) will help to extend the horizontal line from the head out to the vertical line on the paper. Then mark off the number of head lengths within the total height measurement. Begin at the head and mark equivalent head lengths. Count the head lengths and notice the placement of body points (e.g., waist, elbow, knees, wrists).
      3. Compare the differences in horizontal marks of the two persons being analyzed. A proportion is established by describing the number of head lengths per person (i.e., 7 heads high or $8\frac{1}{2}$ heads high). Then the position of a body point is expressed as $3\frac{1}{2}$ heads and so forth.
      4. Explain how the differences could affect the ABC using each set of proportions.

5

Materials of the ABC

EVERY material has a certain visual potential based upon the characteristics it brings to the ABC. We have looked at the body as a preexisting structure. Now we will discuss materials from the point of view of their potential for visual structure. Our purpose is to understand how we view the ABC, and by understanding its materials, we will begin to think about their influence on visual effect.

The mainstream of materials used for the ABC are physically relatively flat, with more length and width than thickness. These materials are arranged upon the body. Exceptions to the mainstream of materials include crocheting, which may proceed from the linear directly into three-dimensional forms; cosmetics, which may be applied directly to the skin; or metals, which may be poured into cylinders for jewelry or body casts.

A wide range of materials is used on the ABC: They can be woven, knitted, felted. They can be fibers, fur, feathers, wood, metal, plastic. They range from soft to crisp, from transparent to opaque, from matte to shiny, from bright hue to muted. The surface can be one color, or printed with a floral motif or a large single flower, or woven into an allover plaid. All of these characteristics influence the material's potential in the ABC.

To understand the role of the materials in the ABC, the viewer must consider their visual effect first and then examine them. What characteristics

contribute to the result? Examine the ABC closely. Image and preserve the shape of the silhouette. How does the ABC appear to be structured? How does the material influence the ABC? Does the silhouette appear as a rectangle, a triangle, a cylinder? The sources of visual structuring influence the visual effect. The observer needs to be continually aware of these sources of visual structuring.

Sources of visual structuring

The three sources of visual structuring of an ABC include *surface, layout,* and *shadow.* Structuring by *surface* is created by variation of the two-dimensional surface from the varying reflectance of the dye or dyes used or from the variation that can create lines and shapes through printing or weaving. *Layout* involves the three-dimensional variation in the way the surfaces are manipulated to face the observer. *Shadow* structuring occurs because of the varying illumination of the environment, creating light and shadow effects on the form. Shadow can be a direct or indirect influence on the ABC and under ordinary circumstances is influenced by layout and surface structuring.

In a visual form all of these sources of structuring interact; however, it is useful to consider each one separately as we view the ABC. Each can be an important influence in the way the ABC appears to the viewer. Each ABC can involve all three sources of structuring, or one source can be more important in viewing a specific ABC. But the viewer cannot ignore the effect of one on the other and it is useful to be able to analyze the influence of each source. By first separating their effects, the viewer can be aware of the role of each. Eventually the interaction of all three can be understood.

SURFACE STRUCTURING. Surface structuring begins with the characteristics the materials bring with them as two-dimensional surfaces. The surface can be varied in a number of ways that affect the visual outcome of the ABC. It can be colored and defined by hue, value, and intensity. It can be a smooth matte surface, a luminous or a shiny one. It can be smooth and thin or thick with a pile. It

can appear to be textured from printing on the surface or from weaving a number of colored fibers together (fig. 5.1).

Even though surface structure occurs on a two-dimensional surface, the perceptual effect may involve organizing several surface levels or planes. The flat, two-dimensional surface thus appears three-dimensional. The viewer organizes in terms of figure-ground, which creates apparent planar levels. For example, a polka dot on an otherwise smooth surface involves the grouping of polka dots as figure—thus creating two levels, one of figure and one of ground (fig. 5.2a). What is viewed as figure appears to lie above the ground. How far the figure appears above the ground depends upon its clarity, i.e., the distinctness of its edge. The pattern in figure 5.2b does not separate as readily as figure from ground be-

5.1. Surface structure from various sources. *Photos courtesy of University of Minnesota.*

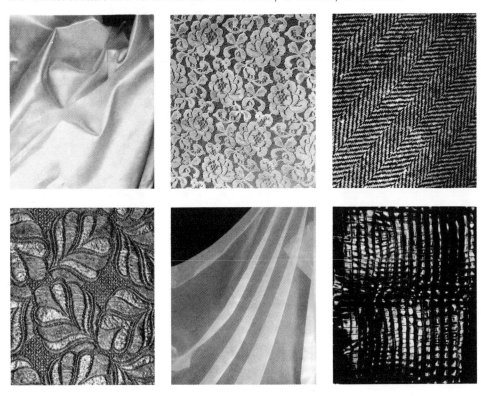

a

b

5.2. **a.** Figure-ground separation from simple enclosed shapes. **b.** Figure-ground integration
from complex shapes. *Photos courtesy of
University of Minnesota; photographer, Leo
Perry.*

5.3. Figure-ground integration–separation from
degree of value contrast. *Photo courtesy of
University of Minnesota.*

cause of the nature of the shapes.

There are some surfaces on which
the figure-ground relation is not separate
and distinct. For example, a pattern may
not separate as figure from the ground
but may make the surface appear somewhat thick and indeterminate (fig. 5.3).
Transparency of surface can create indeterminacy by softening edges (fig. 5.4). A
textured surface often does not separate
into a distinct figure-ground relation. Instead the points separate only somewhat
because of a difference in color and appear to thicken the surface. This occurs
when the textural points create a surface
milling slightly above the ground but not
a distinct figure-ground relation (fig.
5.5a).

A surface that is printed or woven to
include lines and shapes can have a
direction and an order. Figure 5.5b
shows surfaces that direct the eye across
the planar surface. In addition the shapes
in 5.5c group as figure on the ground,
creating depth by planar levels. The

5.4. Transparency of surface can create soft edges. *Designed by Sao (white silk organza architectural blouse). Used by permission.*

larger dark squares group as figure; the small dark squares and light squares in the center of the larger squares can also be viewed as figure. Even though this thickness of surface is apparent and not actually three-dimensional, it influences the spatial organization and visual effect when used in the ABC.

Surfaces can be variously patterned by printing or weaving, producing a range of simple to complex surface structures. Refer to table 1 for a description of a range of simple to complex surface structures. Pattern can derive from an allover, repetitious, simple motif with a clear figure-ground relation (fig. 5.2a). It can be an orderly but indeterminate plaid (fig. 5.6). It can be an allover but irregular and indeterminate motif (fig. 5.7). The surface can involve a border with a simple and distinct figure-ground relation or with a more complex figure-ground relation (fig. 5.8). The surface can also involve a large, complex design

TABLE 1.	*Visual effects of surface structure*
Simple	Smooth matte surface, allover minute points of color
	Irregular pigment or optical mixture of minute points of texture
	Regular repetition of small-sized shapes; large quantity of polka dots, pleats, or gathers; similar value figure-ground integration
	Regular repetition of shapes, small in size, but contrast of value that creates figure-ground separation
	Large-sized shapes, regular repetition, planar levels
Complex	Large-sized shapes, irregular repetition, complex structure of several types of directed viewing; organization both planar and in depth levels

5.5. Surfaces with varying direction and order. **a.** Visual texture creates direction and surface thickness. **b.** Surface direction includes diagonal lines. **c.** Shapes that group as figure creating apparent depth levels. *Photos courtesy of University of Minnesota; photographer, Leo Perry.*

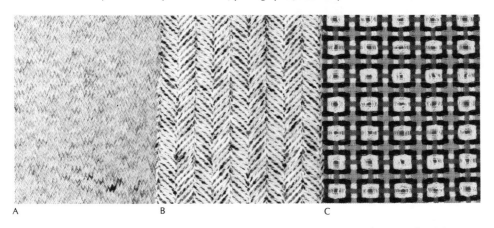

A   B   C

dividing it and creating a structure that is nonrepetitious because its large size would not repeat when used upon the body (fig. 5.9). Size or scale of a surface shape as it relates to the size of the human body is influential in the visual re-

5.6. Regular asymmetric indeterminate plaid. *Photo courtesy of University of Minnesota.*

5.7. Allover, irregular indeterminate surface. *Photo courtesy of University of Minnesota.*

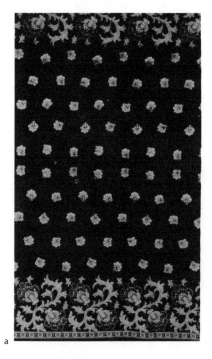

a

b

5.8 Borders with simple, distinct **(a)** and complex **(b)** figure-ground relation. *Photos courtesy of University of Minnesota.*

5.9. Large, complex, nonrepetitious design. *Photo courtesy of University of Minnesota.*

sult of the ABC. Figure 5.10 shows the difference in effect of size and placement of patterns on the same body.

The materials of the ABC can appear simply defined by an allover color on a smooth surface. Then two or three of these materials variously colored can be combined on the body to create a spatial arrangement. Often a surface defined by allover color is also varied with a textural effect, which is part of the weave or knit structure and appears as small protrusions from the surface (fig. 5.11). These protrusions are a microlayout provided by actual three-dimensional surface relief. They can be regular weave or knit patterns, such as the pile of corduroy, or irregular slubs or yarns incorporated into the surface.

Thus the surface structure can include allover repeated surface shapes, irregular repeats, and large singular shapes. The viewer is directed depending upon the nature of the pattern and how it is used in the ABC. The direction of viewing can be horizontal, vertical, or diagonal on the flat surface. In addition the degree of boldness of the pattern influences its priority for the viewer. Stripes that are determinate because of a distinct and hard edge are a visual prior-

5.10.
Patterns of differing size and placement on the same body. **a.** *Photo courtesy of University of Minnesota; designed by Debra Turitto.* **b.** *Photo courtesy of University of Minnesota; designed by Georgia Scheu.*

a

b

5.11. Surface structure created by three-dimensional protrusions. *Photo courtesy of University of Minnesota.*

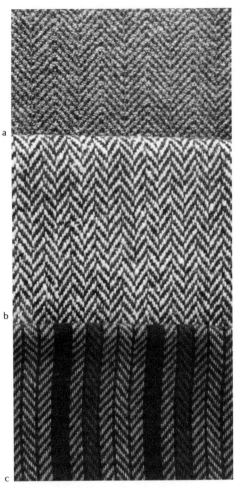

a

b

c

5.12. Indeterminate surfaces with linear direction. *Photo courtesy of University of Minnesota.*

ity for the viewer (fig. 5.10a). Surfaces that also direct the viewer but are more subtle are the indeterminate surfaces in figure 5.12 a and b.

If the spaces between the stripes provide a variation and placement in the ABC encourages it, the viewer can be directed horizontally, across the stripes, or vertically, along the stripe (fig. 5.12 c). A line or shape that changes in some measured aspect such as size or shape can have the result of directing the viewer. When stripes provide a gradation across the stripes from wide to narrower, the potential for directing the viewer is often both horizontal, from one stripe to another, and vertical, along the length of the stripe (fig. 5.13). But the direction of viewing again is influenced when such a surface structure is placed on the body.

The way the surface structure interacts with the body in the layout al-

ways influences its visual effect in the ABC. The shapes created by layout of the ABC can change the visual surface structure. A surface that is geometric and ordered according to the vertical-horizontal of the material could be repeated in layout structuring (fig. 5.14). Such an ordered surface structure could also be used to contradict itself, in a curved shape or on the bias in the ABC. Structuring from surface and layout influence each other and the visual effect of the ABC.

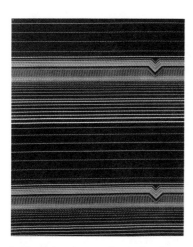

5.13. Stripes in a gradation that directs the viewer. *Photos courtesy of Minneapolis College of Art and Design; designed by Nancy Kirkwood.*

5.14. Structuring from surface and layout influence each other. *Photos courtesy of University of Minnesota; photographer, Leo Perry.*

Thus surface structuring increases the opportunities for combining surfaces to create visual variety. Think how different the visual world would be if it were all beige, smooth surfaces that could be varied only by layout and shadow! Instead colors and textures can define surfaces of the ABC to create spatial effects. This can be accomplished at several stages—by a designer planning the visual effect of the ABC, by a merchandiser displaying the ABC, or by a wearer standing in front of the mirror planning an appearance.

LAYOUT STRUCTURING. Layout structuring involves the physical arrangement of the garment on the body. Layout is created by the three-dimensional manipulation in, out, and around the body of the physical surfaces presented in the ABC. Various materials can be combined and manipulated to create lines and shapes and textural effects. Layout can appear as lines and shapes such as pleats, yokes, collars. Lines and shapes of the silhouette and within the silhouette—such as buttons, pockets, hemlines, the textural effect of soft-edged gathers—are all included in layout (fig. 5.15).

The body structure is three-dimensional and the materials of the ABC are

5 / Materials of the ABC **59**

5.15. ABC showing variety in layout structuring. *Designed by Traci Scherek; photographer, Marty Berglin. Used by permission.*

also three-dimensional when used on the body. But materials may take on many other shapes and lines than just those that follow body conformation. A crisp material can be used to create a shape independent of the body shapes. A soft, thin material can be used to create shapes that interact with the body (fig. 5.16).

When a woven fabric is used in the ABC, the silhouette is affected by the placement of the grain on the body. Grain refers to the warp or filling yarns of the fabric. Lengthwise grain is located at any position along the warp yarn and crosswise grain is at any position along a filling yarn. Bias is using the diagonal of the grain. Lengthwise yarns are kept firmly taut in the weaving process and thus have the least amount of elasticity; the bias is the most elastic. When the lengthwise yarns of the fabric correspond to gravity and are placed on the length of the body they hang straighter and create a more vertical impression than is created when the yarns are placed horizontally on the body. A fabric cut on the bias (diagonally across the grain) often appears to follow body curves more closely.

5.16
The crispness or softness of a material influences shape formation on the body. **a.** Crisp materials can create shapes independent of the body. *Designed by Bonnie Cashin. Used by permission.* **b.** Soft materials can interact with body shapes. *Designed by Bonnie Cashin. Used by permission.*

a   b

5.17. Shapes can be created on the body by draping or cutting and joining shapes. **a.** ABC created by draping folds in material. *Photo courtesy of Minneapolis College of Art and Design; designed by David Walde.* **b.** ABC created by cutting and joining shapes. *Photo courtesy of PBM/ Pincus Brothers-Maxwell, makers of fine men's and women's tailored clothing.*

Two ways to manipulate materials on the body are draping or cutting and joining shapes (fig. 5.17). Draping is the process of incorporating materials on the body, easing to create gathers, bending to create folds, and creasing to create edges, such as tucks. The cutting and joining of pieces also affects the structure and appearance of the ABC. A seamline resulting from the joining of two materials is an important source of line or shape in the viewing of the ABC. Seamlines create lines and shapes such as collars, lapels, and patch pockets, which create a line by enclosing the raw edge of the seam. Sharply defined lines and edges can also be created by hemlines and by materials that are capable of holding a crease or pressed-in edge.

The lines and shapes of layout depend upon the physical nature of the materials. But the physical nature of the materials can be transformed in the ABC. Many different materials can be used, creating a myriad of different visual effects—feathers, coins, leather, or a surface with potential for visual variety in light and shadow effects. The inherent visual character of the material is an important consideration in visual effect (figs. 5.18, 5.19).

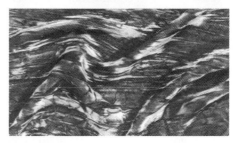

5.18. Inherent character of material influences visual effect. *Photos courtesy of University of Minnesota.*

5.19. Inherent nature of material influences layout. *Designed by Robert Hillestad. Used by permission.*

A one-color surface can be used on the body by itself or in combination by layout with other surfaces. By itself a one-color surface interacts with the colors of the body and the shapes and lines created by layout. Several surfaces can be combined in the layout of an ABC. In addition to the interaction with the colors, lines, and shapes of the body, the color interacts in combination with other colors. An example is the color blocking of spatial areas creating structures and planar levels of organization that can direct our viewing. Viewing can also be directed by bringing together several separate surfaces in gradations of value, intensity, or hue.

In viewing the materials of an ABC, the observer needs to be reminded of the potential for their transformation to the third dimension. Ultimately the way the shapes and surfaces appear on the body in the ABC is more important to the vis-

ual effect than the nature of the flat surfaces. But the potential of the material often depends upon its nature when flat, both its visual surface structure and its manipulability.

A term used to describe the physical nature of many woven and knitted materials is *hand*. Hand actually refers to the way the material feels but is also a way to describe potential for manipulation and includes weight and drape, that is, how the material will hang and fall from the body. Hand influences how the material can be manipulated into various lines and shapes, whether shapes will stand away from the body or cling to it. Certain materials ease very well into small spaces. Some are excellent for pressed pleating because they can maintain a sharp crease, while others can be used only for soft, unpressed pleats.

Their weight influences the way the materials interact with the body. The intimate relation of the weight of material to the silhouette can be demonstrated rather dramatically by altering the physical dimensions of an article of apparel that hangs from the body: for example, the length of a flared skirt. Before hemming, the skirt appears too long when it is tried on. What is viewed in the mirror could be described as follows: all the flares (wedge-shaped folds) interact with the body, are dependent upon the body curves, and the overall effect on silhouette appears quite vertical. But in the process of cutting off several inches and hemming, the silhouette changes. When the skirt is tried on again, it looks much more horizontal. The flares are more independent, much less interrelated with the body curves. How could this happen? The lesser weight reduces the pull of gravity and consequently the silhouette appears different. This type of alteration of visual effect can occur with only slight changes in the physical dimensions of the material.

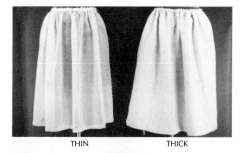

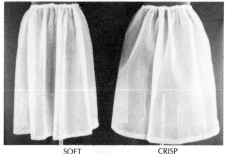

THIN   THICK

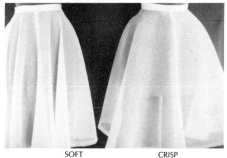

SOFT   CRISP

SOFT   CRISP

5.20. Shape varies in appearance because of fabric that differs. *Photos courtesy of M. DeLong.*

Manipulative characteristics of materials that most affect silhouette have been discussed by Helen Brockman in *The Theory of Fashion Design.* They include the interrelation of the characteristics of soft-crisp and thin-thick. She concludes that the character of the silhouette is influenced by the tactile qualities of the materials chosen. A soft, thin material will create quite a different silhouette from what a crisp, thick one will. As well, a soft, thick material can be manipulated differently than a crisp, thin one can. The visual influence of hand can be very subtle and the viewer needs to experience the influence of all kinds of materials on the body.

The physical dimensions of cut and joined pieces may be identical, but the ABC visually appears quite different when the fabrics used vary in hand (fig. 5.20). A slight change in the degree of crispness or thickness, for example, can affect the visual result of trousers or a skirt. A comparison of two examples reveals some significant visual differences in the interaction with body curves and in the silhouette created.

Many ABCs get their primary identifying character from layout. When we think in terms of some apparel items, such as slacks, dirndl skirt, blazer, or western shirt, we are considering a particular layout structure of lines and shapes on the body. But in layout structuring, the surface is often more than incidental to the visual effect. The viewer must be reminded of its influence on the ABC. For example, garments of similar layout are pictured in figure 5.21, but

5.21. Layout similar, but surface variation creates difference in visual effect. *Photos courtesy of University of Minnesota.*

5.22. Surface definition enhanced by light and shadow effects. *Photo courtesy of University of Minnesota; photographer, Leo Perry.*

what the observer views regarding layout is greatly affected by the way the surface is structured.

LIGHT AND SHADOW STRUCTURING. Surfaces are defined to some degree by reflecting character. They can be matte, luminous, or shiny. A surface may be relatively unstructured in the sense of directing the observer's attention but present a potentially rich source of surface definition greatly enhanced by light and shadow effects (fig. 5.22). The clothed body also offers a source of light and shadow, which, when lighted from a point source, has a potential for casting shadows because of layout (fig. 5.15). A jacket hemline may cast a shadow on the adjacent surface of trousers.

Light and shadow effects may be ignored because of the early perceptual experiences that form our viewing habits. We ignore much light and shadow variation because we have programmed our perception to that which has the most meaning for us, the constancy of our visual world. We ignore those aspects of objects that are not constant; this includes light and shadow. We need to concentrate on how the ABC looks from our immediate visual field to

perceive light and shadow effects. Only when we concentrate on the field immediately in front of us do we actually take notice of what is there. The viewer who ignores light and shadow loses a major source of visual effect of the ABC. In figure 5.23 the shadow carries the viewer's

5.23. Shadow directs the viewer's eye vertically. *Photo courtesy of University of Minnesota; photographer, Leo Perry.*

eye vertically. Reintroducing light and shadow as a variation of a particular visual field can greatly influence the impact of the ABC on the viewer.

Surfaces can be influenced in their capacity to carry light and shadow by their color value (their degree of lightness or darkness). The value of a surface affects its potential as a carrier of light and shadow. A relatively homogeneous light-value surface has different potential for influencing the form than a similar dark-value surface has (fig. 5.24a). A medium-value surface has the most potential for carrying light and shadow effects (fig. 5.24b).

Light and shadow can be controlled when the illumination is directed for special effects. The extent of control in lighting varies since the ABC moves about under normal circumstances. Even though light sources are not usually controlled, an ordinary light source comes from above. Presentation of a costume on a manikin in a gallery would be an exception to this lack of control. Here the light and shadow and resulting visual effect could be staged.

Even though shadow is not ordinarily under complete control, some control can be achieved through the surround in which the ABC occurs. How differently the surfaces of a visual form can appear under different lighting—incandescent, fluorescent, or daylight! Designers have reported their consideration of the different types of street lighting in New York and Paris in selecting surfaces and in designing the layout of an ABC.

Interaction effects

The three sources of structuring—surface, layout, and shadow—all influence the ABC. As sources of structure all can be used to create lines, shapes, colors, and textures. As we consider what contribution each brings to our viewing, we are more aware of what it takes to view all that is in our visual field. The sources of visual structuring need to be separated in viewing the ABC but one or the other may not always take priority. Then it is useful to consider how they interact to create the visual effect (fig. 5.25).

a

b

5.24. Value influences capacity for surface to carry light and shadow. **a.** *Photo courtesy of M. DeLong.* **b.** *Designed by Giorgio Sant'Angelo. Used by permission.*

a   b   c

5.25. Interaction effects of surface, layout, and shadow. **a.** *Photo courtesy of Minneapolis College of Art and Design; designed by Pattie Randall.* **b.** *Photo courtesy of University of Nebraska; student design used by permission of Robert Hillestad.* **c.** *Photo courtesy of University of Nebraska; Gale Warren, designer and model. Used by permission.*

What role does the material play according to its visual effect within the ABC? For example, a textured, tweedy surface used in an ABC can appear to fill the space differently than an allover colored and smooth surface. The textured, tweedy surface appears to thicken the surface and mask seamlines. On the smooth surface the seamline would become more important because the eye would not pause or stop but would proceed quickly to the edge. Of course the areas of color and smooth surfaces and shapes could be affected by other sources of visual structuring.

Materials are defined as two-dimensional surfaces before they are incorporated into the ABC. The qualities of the materials influence their potential in the ABC. A material can appear relatively simple—smooth surface, allover color, medium weight, and midway between soft and crisp in hand. Such a surface can be used for many ABCs. A material with manipulability and no surface structure is often utilized where layout will be emphasized, possibly structured with the layout of pleating, folding, or gathering. The visual effect of the ABCs in figure 5.26 a and b is primarily a result of layout. But the viewer is influenced by the nature of the surface, which can act as a visual carrier of layout. The surface then allows the maximum visual effect from layout.

A surface can be structured with shapes prior to use. The viewer can be directed to the two-dimensional surface in terms of a figure-ground relation or by an indeterminate surface, thus creating a three-dimensional effect. The visual result of an ABC can be influenced by the use of a surface that is structured by distinct shapes. The layout can be masked somewhat because of the priority of such surface structures in viewing (fig. 5.26 c and d).

Thus, even though a surface may be simple or complex in its appearance before its incorporation into the ABC, it may be transformed when it is used (fig. 5.27). A complex structure can appear simpler because of the way it is placed upon the body. Materials with a surface

5.26. **a.** and **b.** Layout primary in the ABC. **a.** *Photo courtesy of Minneapolis College of Art and Design; designed by Mary Deutch.* **b.** *Photo courtesy of Minneapolis College of Art and Design; designed by Karen Heddens.*

a b

c. and **d.** Surface primary in the ABC. **c.** *Photo courtesy of Minneapolis College of Art and Design; designed by Lyneise E. Williams.* **d.** *Photo courtesy of Minneapolis College of Art and Design; designed by Donneen Torrey.*

c d

structure include some with shapes as large as or larger than the body, a situation that greatly influences the layout. An example of such a material is shown in a layout in figure 5.28.

The surface structure can either reveal or camouflage layout. The example in figure 5.29 shows the result of a surface structure with such a strong pattern of irregular shapes that it camouflages some aspects of layout such as body conformation. Layout structure can also

5.27. Layout can influence the visual effect of surface structure. *Photo courtesy of University of Minnesota; photographer, Leo Perry.*

5.28. Size of shape relative to body size influences layout. *Photo courtesy of Minneapolis College of Art and Design; designed by Judy Matthews.*

a   b   c

either reveal or camouflage surface structure.

The ABC can be varied by light and shadow through layout and pigment structuring that can interact with the lighting (fig. 5.15). For example, if the light source is ordinarily from above, a horizontal overlap on a jacket of medium value may produce a shadow most of the time. Photographers can further control this means to create various effects, directing observer viewing by use of different sources of lighting. Shadow effects may be planned in relation to an ordinary light source from above. Layout that utilizes overlapping can be enhanced by shadow from overhead illumination. Thus layout may be revealed by light and shadow.

All sources of visual structuring can define and describe space and therefore direct viewing. Lines can be created by printing or weaving, an effect of surface structure. In layout structure a line can

5.29. Layout structure camouflaged somewhat by surface structure. **a.** *Photo courtesy of Joseph Gazzuolo.* **b.** *Photo courtesy of Fairchild Visuals, division of Fairchild Publications, Inc., New York City.*

a

b

be created by the manipulation of surfaces into edges or by combining two different surfaces. By asking what is the visual effect from each, the observer can assure an awareness and understanding of all sources of structuring in viewing. Lines, shapes, colors, and textures can be made visually distinct or indistinct whether produced by pigment on the two-dimensional surfaces of the ABC or created through layout and/or light and shadow effects.

Even though the visual effect of materials has been emphasized, the influence of the tactile and kinesthetic aspects of surfaces also needs to be discussed. Our experience with materials is more than just visual and this influences how the viewer responds to the visual.

INFLUENCE FROM TACTILE AND KINESTHETIC EXPERIENCES. Visual, tactile, and kinesthetic experiences all affect our viewing of the ABC. Many of our important early sensory experiences are tactile. A child likes very much to touch soft things—soft blankets, furry stuffed animals. The tactile qualities of materials mean much to us and later give meaning

to our visual sense. Kinesthetic experiences that influence viewing also occur in our childhood. The weight of a coat is experienced as different from that of a cotton shirt. The legs interact with a long dress or robe as we walk. How exciting it is to twirl the body in a long nightgown and feel the circle of the hem extend outward and then momentarily swirl against the body!

Though the visual aspects of materials and the way they can interact in viewing are primary considerations, our other senses are very much present in visual interpretation. A sweater may be viewed as soft because we have previously experienced its softness by touch. Other materials offer a similar relation between visual and tactile experiences. For example, a suede leather surface that feels soft and somewhat furry also looks shaded with light and dark areas on the surface. This similarity of visual and tactile message needs to be recognized as a large part of the pleasure we gain in viewing materials.

However, a surface may differ in its visual and tactile character. Often, touching will reveal a discrepancy from how the surface visually appears. For example, a sequined surface visually is shiny. When touched it does not feel smooth and slippery as one would expect if a direct correspondence between tactile and visual experiences always existed. In this case the tactile and visual offer two quite different sensory experiences.

A printed surface is another example of a surface that appears different from the way it feels. Many types of definition can be printed onto the surface, thereby altering it visually but changing the tactile character minimally.

Materials are also influenced visually because of their kinesthetic relation to the body. How the material hangs from the body is a factor that not only influences our judgment about wearing certain materials but also may influence our viewing. Wool may look scratchy and heavy because of the way it feels and moves on the body, while silk looks and feels smooth and moves and hangs differently on the body. The way wool and silk interact with the body can certainly influence the viewing. Empathizing with the wearer because of our past experience with the kinesthetic aspects of a material affects our visual perception of that material. This is when we make such comments as, "That looks like it would feel scratchy!"

It is important to distinguish between the visual, tactile, and kinesthetic qualities of materials. While we can recognize the associations of the visual with the tactile and the visual with the kinesthetic, separating them in our awareness is useful and ultimately leads to a greater understanding of the visual nature of the ABC.

Visual exercises

I. Understanding the influence of hand on the potential of a material to relate to the ABC.
   A. Watch a person tailor a jacket. How is the material being shaped? Study the surface of the material. Handle it. (Grasp the material between the thumb and fingers. Lift it gently and let it fall, observing it all the while.) Describe as follows: (1) the hand and (2) the softness or crispness and thinness or thickness.
   B. Observe a person making a bridal gown. What are the differences from the jacket in A in how the material is being shaped? Study the surface of the material. Handle it. Describe the nature of the material (as in A above).
   C. Compare the materials from A and B, if possible in completed ABCs. What qualities of the materials influence visual effect?
   D. Using this awareness of the relation between the tactile and visual, find fabric swatches that could be used for different visual effects. Find photos of ABCs for which the fabrics could be used. Describe how they would be viewed. Consider whether the results would be determinate or indeterminate, flat or rounded, examples of planar integration or separation, examples of clothing priority or body priority.

II. Relating fabric to ABC.
   A. Select three fabrics or other materials for use in an ABC. (Refer to each fabric by an attached number.) Analyze the potential of each of your fabrics for the ABC using the following guide:
      1. Sources of structure.
         a. Describe material with regard to visual texture, weave structure, etc. Does it look light or heavy, open or compact, rough or smooth?
         b. Describe fabric hand. Is it soft or crisp, thin or thick, light or heavy, springy or limp, pliable or stiff, stretchy or nonstretchy?
         c. What is the silhouette capability, that is, will it create its own shape? Will it conform to the body? Could it be used for a closed or for an open form?

d. Is the fabric capable of carrying details of tailoring or those of a draped type of ABC? Will it manipulate into pockets, pleats, gathers? Will these details be visually apparent on the surface of the ABC?

e. Describe the fabric surface as to color, degree of surface variation. Are there shapes? If so, describe. Are the shapes large or small, regular or irregular, orderly or random, clear or blurred, two-dimensional or three-dimensional? Does the fabric have a direction and/or pattern (e.g., border, stripe, plaid)?

f. How can the fabric be used in the ABC? What is its potential in an organization? (For example, if it has direction or pattern is its use limited? If so, how? Imagine several possible uses.)

g. Will the fabric allow light and shadow? Will placing it on a form change its character? Will construction parts such as collar and pockets be noticeable? Is it shiny or dull, opaque or transparent?

2. Sources of meaning. Describe briefly what associations you make with the fabric. (How have you seen it used before? What does it bring to mind?)

3. What is the capability of each fabric in relation to the other fabrics? (Does one advance and one recede? Does the combination make blending or contrasting edges?)

B. Plan for ABC.

1. Plan an organization that will place the fabrics on the body. Roughly block out and plan for placement of areas of fabrics.

2. Describe how you have utilized specific fabric characteristics in organizing your ABC. Use your analysis from A to aid in determining visual effect.

3. Describe how you have treated the body visually in terms of lines, shapes. What is figure and what is ground? Does your plan emphasize parts or whole first?

6

The visual definers

THE visual definition of the ABC includes those layout and surface aspects that characterize the part—these are line, shape, point, texture, and color. They function to provide perceptual definition of the visual part. A visual part is defined by edge and surface. Whether the visual part is viewed primarily as defined by edge or by surface is based on the relations of the visual definers. Used in combination in the ABC, definers can create an infinite variety of visual effects.

Visual structuring (discussed in chap. 5) can arise from such sources as two-dimensional surfaces and from three-dimensional layout of the surfaces on the body. However, identifying the source of structure does not adequately describe the visual effect. Other relationships affect the character of the ABC. For example, a line may be either hard edged or soft edged from several sources of structuring. A line printed on the surface of a material can produce a hard edge or the layout of a hemline can produce a hard edge. A soft edge may also be created from several sources—shadow, surface, or layout. Whether a line is hard or soft edged is important to the visual character of the ABC.

The visual definers offer the potential for visual relationships within the ABC. In the discussion of visual relations in chapter 2, degree of similarity was shown to be an important characteristic of a part that could result in the observer relating it to another part. The observer tends to group similar aspects of parts and segregate dissimilar aspects.

Parts in the ABC can be similar in many ways. There are characteristics of shapes that interrelate and can be grouped, such as circles with other circles. But shapes can also be similar in color. Blue circles group with other blue circles in a simple organization, but what happens when some circles are blue and some are red, or there are blue circles and blue squares? Do they still group when they are similar in some aspects but dissimilar in others?

Visual relationships can derive from many characteristics of definers, for example, long or short lines, hard-edged or soft-edged shapes, light- or dark-value colors, red or blue hues. Some of these relations are direct and quantifiable, while others are the result of sensory order and may provide a visual relationship via contrast from a sensory opposite. Such a case would be the visual relationship occurring from color complements. The viewer can either perceive the relation of complementary hues used within one composition or as a result of visual fatigue perceive the complement in an afterimage.

Thus to fully understand the ABC, it is not enough to identify visual relationships without understanding the reasons for them. How we prioritize in the process of viewing is better understood if we can separate and describe the way the ABC gains definition. Understanding the nature of the visual definers and how they can provide visual relations is the topic for the following discussion.

LINEAR DEFINITION

Linear definition is that of line and edge and derives from lines, shapes, and sometimes point. The characterization of an ABC can result from the dominance of linear definition. Regardless of how dominant it is, as we organize the ABC, it influences how the ABC will look.

Visual definition of the ABC cannot be limited to just the clothing ensemble. The entire apparel-body construct must be our frame of reference and this extends to any discussion of visual definers. For example, the visual effect of a line at the neck is not just a result of the line of the clothing but also of the interaction with the neck itself and the hair shape and the shape of the body.

becomes very wide we may call it a shape. A very wide line usually appears as a shape unless its main function is directing.

Line can be described as straight, angular, curved, or folded. Line can define the flat surface or the folds of a three-dimensional surface. Line can be described as regular or irregular, distinct or indistinct, direct or indirect. A line may curve in one direction and be a simple curved line or in several directions and be a compound curve. A curve may be shallow and flattened or full and rounded. If the curve of a line comes close to itself, visually it may be perceived as shape.

Lines can be perceived in terms of an in-out space, relatively close to or far away from the observer. For example, line can vary in character from decisive and sharp, as in pressed pleats, to intermittent and soft, as in gathers. It can

Line

VISUAL FUNCTION. The function of line in the whole can be to provide visual interest, as do pleats in a yoke; to give direction, as do a row of buttons at center front that the observer connects as a line; or to divide space, as does the edge of a jacket, especially if the jacket contrasts in some respect (such as shape, color, or texture) with what is adjacent to it or is emphasized by light and shadow. A single dominant line can become an important focus in taking in the ABC (fig. 6.1). Numerous lines creating a pattern on a surface can become textural in effect (fig. 6.2).

GENERAL APPEARANCE. Line in the ABC is identified by its length and by the ratio of its length to its width. To recognize a line, the observer must perceive its length and thinness. If a line

6.2. Numerous lines create surface pattern. *Photo courtesy of University of Nebraska; Marv Graff, designer; Gale Warren, model. Used by permission.*

6.1. A single dominant line in an ABC can create focus and direction for the viewer. *Photo courtesy of University of Minnesota; Adrian Retrospective.*

appear thick or thin. A thick line boldly contrasting with its surround can appear closer to the observer than a thin line does.

CONTINUOUS OR DISCONTINUOUS. A continuous line, one that does not change direction quickly, is more easily viewed than a discontinuous line, one that abruptly changes direction or is interrupted (fig. 6.3). The discontinuous line will often attract focus to a visual part (fig. 6.4). However, it is usually the point of discontinuity that creates the focus. On the other hand, a line that is continuous and connects several shapes is a source of similarity and visual connection within the ABC.

DIRECTION. Directing the visual path is an important characteristic of line and an awareness of it is vital in viewing the ABC (fig. 6.1). Eye movements while taking in the visual form are the source of the sensation of direction. The observer's bodily movements and tensions may also be a source of directing, as when an observer traces the curved lines of the body with the hands in midair. The observer is literally feeling the tension of movement and putting his body movements into the viewing process.

LENGTH. The length of a line is important to the way it is viewed: a shorter line is more immediately viewed but may not direct viewing because of its short length. A longer line may direct viewing because it is not all taken in with one glance.

The length of a line in the context of the body and clothing is also significant. If the line is just as long as a body part or appears to continue a body part, it may be less noticed than a longer or shorter one. For example, a hat brim that extends horizontally beyond the widest

6.3. An ABC with a long continuous line can connect body parts. *Photo courtesy of Minneapolis College of Art and Design; designed by Denise Boozer.*

6.4. An ABC with discontinuous line will often attract focus to a visual part. *Photo courtesy of University of Minnesota, Goldstein Gallery.*

part of the head offers contrast and potential focus.

A line may begin and end in one body view or extend around the body. In the context of the body straight lines can be vertical, horizontal, or diagonal. A diagonal line often appears to extend around the body. Vertical lines usually can be taken in within one body view and horizontal lines can be seen as related to one body view or as extended around the body. If a horizontal line is viewed as an edge of a shape and as a part of the visual field, it relates to one body view.

ACTUAL OR IMPLIED. A line connection can be actual or implied, actual when the eye of the observer traces a continuous seamline or stripe printed on the surface and implied when two points of interest with relatively clear space between them are connected visually (e.g., a path from one button to another).

LINE OR EDGE. Line may be perceived primarily as line or as edge. Line as line is distinguished as figure on top of ground (fig. 6.5), whereas line as edge is usually perceived as the boundary for a shape, belonging more to one adjacent shape than to another (fig. 6.6). This comprehension of line as edge may occur when the line becomes important

in the observer's viewing, for example, in the process of viewing a transition between one part and another (fig. 6.7).

6.6. Line may become an edge of a shape. *Photo courtesy of University of Minnesota, Goldstein Gallery.*

6.7. The buttons continue the center front line as well as integrate the black and white areas. *Photo courtesy of University of Minnesota, Goldstein Gallery.*

6.5. Line may be perceived as figure on ground. *Designed by Yvonne Karlsson. Used by permission.*

6 / The visual definers   **75**

Edges are related to area of shapes, but it is useful to separate the idea of edge because at times the edge of a large shape is perceived in the focusing process more as edge than as a portion of the shape. For example, hemlines are often considered in viewing as edge first and secondly as part of a shape.

HARD EDGE OR SOFT EDGE. Lines that are simple, angular, decisive, and sharp are called hard edged (fig. 6.8), and lines that are curving, indistinct, and blurred are called soft edged (fig. 6.9). Hard and soft edges affect the character of an ABC because of the way the observer takes them in. Hard edges are often accompanied by other factors influencing perception that result in a primacy and an immediacy in viewing, such as smooth, seemingly unfilled surfaces. Soft edges are often accompanied by filled or textured surfaces, light and shadow, or

6.9. Lines that are curving and indistinct are soft edged. *Photo courtesy of University of Minnesota, Goldstein Gallery; photographer, Judy Olausen.*

transparent surfaces. Soft edges often do not attract our attention to edge, rather to surface or to light and shadow incorporated by the soft edge (fig. 6.10).

6.8. Lines that are simple, angular, and distinct are hard edged. *Designed by Yvonne Karlsson. Used by permission.*

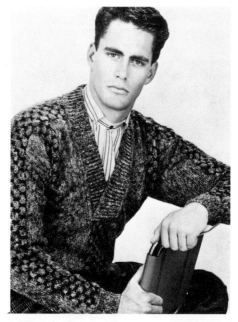

6.10. Soft edges are often accompanied by filled or textured surfaces. *Photo courtesy of Jhane Barnes; photographer, Albert Bray.*

POSITION. Line is characterized by its position (fig. 6.11). Position includes the line's relationship to the body, to adjacent space (left-right, up-down), and its apparent distance from the observer (in-out, near-far). Thick, soft-edged lines appear farther away from the observer and thick, hard-edged lines appear closer.

Where a line is located on the body is important to the way it is viewed. Since the body is basically vertical, vertical lines may reinforce body verticality. They can relate closely to the visual axis of the body, as in the case of a center front line created by a button closing at center front. Horizontal lines draw attention away from the body verticality and may divide the body, depending upon their position. A bikini may be viewed as horizontal lines or as shapes on the body.

The observer's perceptual habits influence the viewing of position. Many common eye movements such as those used reading books or clocks are from left to right; this association affects our perception. So we often view the body from left to right and come to anticipate this direction when viewing the position of lines on the body. Any lines that require an eye movement contrary to reading require more energy and consequently may be associated with more aggressiveness and energy.

SOURCES

SEAMS. Seamlines are the lines made when two pieces of material are stitched together, usually enclosing or covering seam edges. Seams as lines can vary in importance in the context of the ABC. The seamline itself can be less important in perception when it is primarily functioning to create shape. It can be important when located at a body position that is being emphasized. For example, a seamline is more important at center front of the body when it is accompanied by stripes placed at an angle creating a chevron effect. An enclosed seam can be visually important when defining a lapel that happens to be fashionable or timely.

A seamline may overlap another surface. If the surface is capable of reflecting light and dark, the resulting fold can become more emphatic through the increased definition provided by shadow.

6.12.
Lines can be folds of material in the ABC. *Photo courtesy of University of Minnesota; designed by Georgia Scheu.*

FOLDS. Many of the materials of the ABC are very pliable and this characteristic is utilized in creating its visual effect. By easing or gathering a long piece of material into a short space many visual effects can be achieved. One is the creation of lines from the gathers. A fold or pleat can be a source of line that may either be short or long, extending the length of a shape. For example, trouser pleats may be the result of the relation of the fit of a small area, the difference in circumference between hip and waist, and thus only extend to the hip. Trouser pleats may also extend the length of the trousers in a distinct full-length crease. To extend without interruption requires avoidance of the body curvatures.

Folds can be soft edged or hard edged. Soft edges can be folds created by a shallow in-and-out curve, which can then be further defined by light and shadow (fig. 6.12). Hard edges can be the fold created by an enclosed seam at a jacket hemline or a lapel or collar edge. Some materials can retain a permanent crease, which can be utilized in a pleat with a distinct and crisp edge.

PIGMENT. Surfaces can be structured by printing colors, which creates line, or by weaving several colors side by side to create line (fig. 6.13). These lines often appear in repetition in stripes or plaids. Lines created in this way can be visually as important in the ABC as line from other sources. The line can be soft when two colors close in value are used. Two

6.13. Surfaces structured by pigment can create lines. *Designed by Yvonne Karlsson. Used by permission.*

tints or light values can be placed side by side and create soft edges. Line from pigment can also be used for hard edges, as in a black and white variation that creates a figure-ground separation.

IN COMBINATION. When a number of lines are placed together, their grouping needs to be considered (fig. 6.14). The eye can jump between two lines varying in length or in some other measured difference such as width or distance apart. Awareness of the visual path is important because the eye may follow the actual line or notice its difference from other lines.

A grouping of lines creates a grid effect when two sets of parallel lines cross each other. If the lines are all otherwise equal in such aspects as width and color, no hierarchy is created. Then the lines appear grouped as figure on ground, or if a square is created by the lines it can become figure. In this way a checkered surface is often ambiguous because the observer can view it as reversible figure to ground (refer to section on planar separation or integration, chap. 3, for discussion).

A hierarchy may be created if some of the lines in a group are made visually more important. Superimposing lines on top of other lines is a way of making them visually more important. Varying the lines in thickness or boldness can create sets of lines that lead the observer into the surface. Plaids are often viewed as having a depth or thickness of surface because of a planned order of in-out or depth viewing.

AS A SOURCE OF ASSOCIATED MEANING. Line character may be associated with characterization of object or event (figs. 6.8, 6.9, 6.10, 6.15). A simple and direct line as related to the body and clothing shapes is immediately and easily seen. Thus in a situation of business associated with seriousness and directness, the straight line is more often used because it connotes a simple directness. In sportswear a message of activity can be conveyed by the use of angular, discontinuous, or straight lines. A curving or soft, full line, such as a ruffle on a shirt or a curve created by a full sleeve, is often used in evening wear. The softening of line is associated with

6.14. Lines in combination must be considered as they relate to each other. *Designed by Yvonne Karlsson. Used by permission.*

6.15. Line character can be associated with various meanings in the ABC. **a.** *Photo courtesy of Andrew Fezza Menswear; photographer, Thom Gilbert.* **b.** *Photo courtesy of Minneapolis College of Art and Design; designed by Lyneise E. Williams.*

a   b

an event that encourages visual lingering.

PRIORITY. As the observer views and analyzes the ABC, priority of line is considered within the ABC and in comparison with line in other ABCs. This determines how line helps to characterize the visual effect. The observer needs to understand line priority to adequately describe its effect. This also involves an assessment of line direction and position.

INTERACTION. When a striped, printed surface is in the ABC, it will be interrupted by other sources of line, e.g., folds, seamlines. Visual priority can be created by changing the direction of line on the body, by changing the pattern of stripes, by folding in on some potential visual parts and not others (fig. 6.16).

Shape

VISUAL FUNCTION. The function of shape in the ABC can range from providing a source of figure to a source of ground. When shapes are small in size, numerous, and regular, such as polka

6.16.
Lines interact in layout by changing direction or pattern of stripes. **a.** *Designed by Yvonne Karlsson. Used by permission.* **b.** *Photo courtesy of University of Minnesota; designed by Amy Gerlinger.*

a   b

dots, they can be viewed as an area of visual texture or pattern. Shape can be the source of many types of visual parts in the ABC. Shapes can be the focus of attention when singular and isolated from other shapes. A small bold shape in isolation often becomes a focal point. A large shape that occupies space distinctly and boldly is viewed as a priority part (fig. 6.17, *color section*).

GENERAL APPEARANCE. Shape is perceived as a bounded area or as a definitive outline with or without a defining surface. If the surface of a shape is similar to its surround, it is defined by outline. The outline can become figure. A shape whose surface is different from its surround may be primarily defined by surface. Then the shape as figure is the surface of the shape and ground is the adjacent surround that appears to lie under it. Thus the figure-ground relation is different in these two instances (fig. 6.18).

Shapes within the ABC may be categorized as organic, that is, bounded by fluid curves, or geometric. They may be categorized as regular or irregular. Regular shapes are bounded by straight or curved lines and are often viewed as simple figures separated from ground. Irregular shapes may be bounded by straight *and* curved lines and are often

a.

shared contour

shape perceived as bounded by outline

shape filled

b.

discontinuous-overlapping contours

6.18. **a.** Shapes that touch at an edge have shared contours. Shapes can appear filled or banded by an outline. **b.** Shapes that overlap can appear as a figure-ground relation with the continuous shape appearing as figure.

viewed as integrated figure to ground. Regular and geometric shapes are usually simpler to perceive than irregular and organic shapes (fig. 6.19).

The entire ABC is the viewing reference when identifying shapes. Shapes within the silhouette can include the head and the shapes created by the

6.19. Shape may be (*left to right*) regular, irregular, geometric, or organic. Regular and geometric shapes are often easier to perceive.

6.20. Shapes that are similar in character and repeat in the ABC group for the viewer. *Designed by Traci Scherek; photographer, Marty Berglin. Used by permission.*

hair, eyeglasses, makeup, jewelry. Earrings, for example, can define a new shape apart from the head shape or repeat the head shape. The head shape can close at the chin or extend beyond to include the neck. The shape of a neckline can group or separate the head and upper torso (fig. 6.20).

SIMPLE TO COMPLEX. Simple shapes of the ABC include the circle, square, triangle, and rectangle. Simple shapes have continuous or definite contours. Simple shapes are easily viewed and occur frequently as pockets, buttons, cuffs and in surface shapes such as polka dots (when large enough to be perceived as circles and not points).

More complex shapes might be the shape of a jacket or a hand. When such shapes are adjacent, they may have discontinous or shared contours. They are difficult to view as visual parts. Some

shapes become bounded or enclosed by the interaction of a seamline with the body. For example, the head and neck may appear to become figure, or a source of focus, because of a neckline. This would be a shared contour, that is, the edge could be viewed as belonging to either the neck of the body or to the apparel. A discontinous contour often occurs because of overlap of one shape with another. This creates depth levels and complexity of shape.

Complex shapes within the silhouette include an upper torso shape such as a jacket or shirt or a lower torso shape such as pants or skirt or legs and shoes. These shapes can include within them other layout shapes such as pockets, collars, cuffs or printed surface shapes such as a floral pattern. To what degree these shapes take on importance as parts depends upon their nature—color and texture, difference from

a   b

6.21. **a.** Planar shapes make the ABC appear smooth and flat, especially when edges contrast. *Photo courtesy of Donna Karan, New York; photographer, Pierre Sherman.* **b.** Depth shape emphasizes the three-dimensional character of the surface. *Photo courtesy of Kleibacker historic costume collection; 1930s bias-cut wedding dress.*

adjacent visual parts, simplicity and clarity of boundary.

As a shape becomes larger and more complex the outline may become less important in our perception, and other aspects will take on importance, such as how its surface is defined. The shape may be noted for its similarity to the silhouette shape or for its direction related to the visual axis of the body.

PLANAR. Planar means flat, and even though the body is a rounded surface, there are shapes that appear smooth and flat on it. Shapes may be small and positioned on the body so that the surface appears relatively flat, with the boundary an important characteristic. An example is a patch pocket positioned close to the center front axis of the body. When a surface is devoid of interest or has a highly contrasting edge, the three-dimensional nature of the body may not be noticed (fig. 6.21a). Then the main visual characteristic of the shape will be its outline. This can occur for a small shape within the ABC or for the entire silhouette of the costume. This phenomenon is viewed and remembered as a flattened cookie cutter effect.

DEPTH. Some shapes on the body appear to be rounding. A dirndl skirt emphasizes the three-dimensional character of the surface. Depth shape is viewed when a shape appears to be contoured either by the body or through the manipulation of the surface to create gathers and folds (fig. 6.21b). A slim, close-to-the-body skirt with a small regular print calls attention to the surface as a rounding protrusion from its silhouette. Depth shape is also viewed when the surface appears thick because of a pile such as fur or tweed filled with minutely varying points. Additionally, a surface that is flat can appear thick because of a pattern printed on the surface.

POSITION. Important to shape is its use in relation to the body—its size, number, position, and direction (fig. 6.22). A circular shape can be one large pin positioned near the head or a number of small buttons in a row featured down the center front or diagonally across the shoulder. Circular shapes may appear to be randomly placed or ordered.

A shape may have an inherent direction such as a rectangle does. When positioned on the body it may coincide with the verticality of the body or extend horizontally across the body.

A shape may be viewed in its entirety within one body view or be completed only if viewed as it rounds the body. A circular shape can be closed all in one body view or encircle the body. In the latter case the observer sees only a portion of the circle from one position. From prior experience we know, however, that a belt encircles the body cylinder, and we can close the circle in our mind.

SOURCES OF SHAPE

SILHOUETTE. A most basic shape of the ABC is the silhouette, which can provide a frame of reference for our perception of all its other shapes. The silhouette is the outer perimeter of the entire form. Its character can be very defined and bold

6.22. Shapes in their use in the ABC can vary as to position, size, direction. **a.** *Ronaldus Shamask's "Chevron Ensemble" in a combination of swiss cotton and silk organza, spring/summer 1983. Used by permission.* **b.** *Photo courtesy of Chou Chou, St. Paul, Minnesota.*

a   b

or undefined and subtle. It is important to note the silhouette, its shape and character, because it can serve as a reference for all of the associations of the remaining parts. As a shape the silhouette can repeat the basic verticality of the body or take on new shapes, apart from the body silhouette. It can appear to be enclosing the body, to be a relatively closed form, or seem open to the surrounding space.

A silhouette that is boldly defined will detach from the surround. Attention then is easily focused within the form. Some clothing attracts attention because of bold clear-cut boundaries, such as a black suit that provides an immediate focus within the ABC (fig. 6.21a). Other types of clothing, such as an evening gown, may appear more open or interrelated with surround, inviting a less immediate focus, a softness, and a visual lingering.

LAYOUT. Shapes may be created from folds of material that hang from the shoulders or waistline. These shapes vary from primarily tubular to triangular, or A-shaped. Shapes from layout are sleeves, pockets, lapels, necklines; and these shapes can be simple or complex to view (fig. 6.23a).

PIGMENT. Shapes may be printed on the surface (fig. 6.23b). Such shapes take on many different characteristics. They can appear to be small isolated figures on a large expanse of ground or a large single figure. Shapes can appear to blend with the ground (planar integration) or stand away boldly and distinctly from the ground (planar separation). They can be grouped on one level as figure above the ground or on several levels.

Pattern is a term used for shapes that define the surface through repetition. A pattern may be simple, small, clearly bounded shapes repeated intermittently

a

b

6.23. **a.** Shapes may be created from folds of material in layout. *Ronaldus Shamask's "Cello Jacket," linen woven sash by Jeffrey Aronoff for Shamask, spring/summer 1981; photo by Harlan Layden. Used by permission.* **b.** Shapes may be created from prints on the surface. *Photo courtesy of Albert Nipon Co., Inc.*

as figure on ground. Such a pattern may give surface definition but not enter into the part-to-whole relation of the ABC. Instead such definition can be part of the determinate-indeterminate character of the surfaces. Pattern may also be large shapes that must be considered in the part-to-whole relation.

AS A SOURCE OF ASSOCIATED MEANINGS. Shapes can echo the meaning associated with line, e.g., a shape that is simple and direct is often associated with business. A shape can direct the eye and thus imply meaning; e.g., if it repeats body verticality it can be associated with stateliness. Repetition of shapes that are regular and geometric, as in a plaid, is often associated with order and stability, whereas repetition of irregular or organic shapes is associated with disorder and excitement.

PRIORITY. Whether the shapes of the layout or the shapes printed on the surface become a viewing priority depends upon the relative strength of each; a visual dominance depends upon how a shape relates to other shapes within the ABC. It can be a singular contrast and immediately perceived as focus or one of many repetitious shapes. The following are characteristics of a shape that can make it a primary visual part: distinctly defined surface, isolation of single shape, hard-defined edge, simple outline, continuous edge, no shared or overlapping edges.

INTERACTION. A shape printed on the two-dimensional surface and placed within the ABC can be interrupted by the layout of the silhouette as it extends around the body cylinder. Shapes printed on the surface are often interrupted when placed upon the body. They can be interrupted by gathers or folds or pockets.

Perception of the outline of a shape can be altered by surface. When a bounded area is filled with visual texture, the observer can become more aware of surface than edge definition. Then the surface appears to have depth, a thickness and energy not present in a surface that appears smooth and devoid of texture. Shapes are often characterized by the dominance of either their surface or their edge.

Point

VISUAL FUNCTION. The function of the point in perception is assessed within its context—the ABC. The point may be observed as the focus of a primary visual part, the point of the V of a neckline or hairline. Thus, it may be important as a discontinuity or contrast in the visual path. It may define a more obscure aspect of the surface or a continuous direction of a line, as one of a row of buttons. Whether a point is singular in focus or is better described as one minute aspect interacting with numerous other points can be observed from its context.

GENERAL APPEARANCE. Point in perception defines location on the body and position in space (fig. 6.24). Thus it may be included in a discussion of linear or surface definition depending upon its number. A single point can vary in importance based upon its context. A large number of points can be textural, while a single point can be a significant visual focus. In the ABC a point often implies a convergence of two lines. Two lines that cross often create a point of focus at the crossing or a shape containing an angle whose tip may be viewed as a point.

ONE-POINT FOCUS. Viewing a critical point in our perception may involve

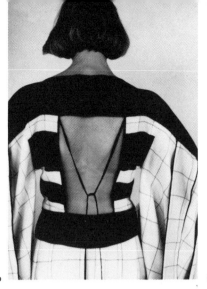

6.24. Point in the ABC defines a location on the body and varies from a one-point focus to many points, which define a space. **a.** *Designed by Yvonne Karlsson. Used by permission.* **b.** *Designed by Yvonne Karlsson. Used by permission.* **c.** *Photo courtesy of University of Minnesota, Goldstein Gallery.*

taking in several parts of the ABC or only one of its visual parts. A visual point can be as precise and explicit as the tip of a stickpin or button or as implicit as a portion of the silhouette that involves two lines meeting, such as the horizontal line of the shoulder and the vertical of the arm or the two legs of trousers at the crotch.

MANY POINTS. To the observer the point in perception can be many points creating surface effects such as polka dots do. Then the point can serve to define a planar surface. If polka dots are covering the surface, the observer tends to perceive their redundancy as order, consistently affecting the surface on a second level of dots above the surface—figure on ground. Even though we tend to perceive them as constant, consider the variations in perceiving a polka dot on the surface of a material that covers the body. The polka dot can be placed on any one of a number of areas of the body, covered by a fold or gather, interrupted by a seam, shaded by light and shadow, or mistaken for a freckle.

PRIORITY OF POINT. The focal point is a primary visual part and usually captures our attention immediately. To do so requires contrast from the surround and as such it usually appears to be figure on top of ground. A point often becomes a focus when it is located strategically along the visual axis of the ABC, reinforcing or contradicting other important lines or shape. Asymmetrical treatment may occur because the differential weighting of two focal points on the body creates a tension between them.

SURFACE DEFINITION

Surface definition is the characterization of the surface of a shape. Surface is defined by texture and color. A primary visual function of both texture and color is definition of spatial position.

Surface texture

VISUAL FUNCTION. Surface texture can provide interest for the ABC because it varies the surface. It also has potential for providing spatial position for visual parts within a whole. Surface texture can provide a near or far away effect for the observer when the surface is variously defined. It can provide a direction for the observer when, for example, surface parts are textured in a gradation effect from smooth to rough. When a surface appears active and very full, it can take priority over edge definition.

GENERAL APPEARANCE. Surface texture refers to the surface variation of a shape. The word *texture* is derived from the Latin for weaving and since many of the materials of the ABC are woven, it is appropriately applied to these surfaces. However, surface texture includes more than just evidence of weaving.

Textured or textural usually refers to surface appearance created through minute variations. When point becomes many points, it defines a surface as textured. *Microlayout* is a term for the three-dimensional effect of surfaces from such sources as knitting or weaving but also from fringe, knots, and other applied protrusions. A single protrusion does not usually create focus, but a group of protrusions can attract attention to surface (fig. 6.25). Visual texture is not limited to minute woven-surface variations. Visual texture may include shimmering highlights and shadows from a reflecting surface or the projections and hollows from folds of fabric (fig. 6.24c). Even if the surface is printed, it may still appear to be textured, as in the case of very minute points of color printed overall.

In the ABC the surfaces can vary from

6.25. Multiple points and microlayout create a textured surface. **a.** *Designed by Bonnie Cashin. Used by permission.* **b.** *Photo courtesy of Fairchild Visuals, division of Fairchild Publication, Inc., New York City.*

a

b

6.30. The orange-red and blue-green of this ABC are complementary. *Photo courtesy of Minneapolis College of Art and Design; designed by David Walde.*

6.17. Shapes to note are the angular shapes of the shoulder, the bracelet, the belt, the hem, and the pleats; rounded shapes include the surface pattern, hair, earrings, sleeves, and shoes. *Designed by Traci Scherek; photographer, James Gallop. Used by permission.*

6.32. Complementary colors used in less intensity can appear subtle. *Designed by Traci Scherek; photographer, Kevin Peterson. Used by permission*

6.33. Differences in hue, value, and intensity can affect spatial position of surfaces and direct the eye. *Photo courtesy of Minneapolis College of Art and Design; designed by Karla Kritz; modeled by Candy Kuehn.*

a

b

9.4. Designer Traci Scherek through color expresses **a.** Calm and delicate. *Designed by Traci Scherek; photographer, Kevin Peterson. Used by permission.* **b.** Calm and strong. *Designed by Traci Scherek; photographer, James Gallop. Used by permission.*

6.26. Visual texture from a thick, long pile may create its own surface and affect shape. **a.** *Photo courtesy of Joseph Gazzuolo.* **b.** *Designed by Bonnie Cashin. Used by permission.* **c.** *Designed by Robert Hillestad; Michele Winkler Minnick, model. Used by permission.*

b   c

smooth to rough, fine to coarse, even to uneven, soft to hard, matte to shiny, transparent to opaque, heavy to light, dense to spaced. A surface usually is noticed because it appears to have some variation not distinguishable as shape.

Textured surfaces within the ABC include the skin surface and the light and dark effects that the hair can provide. Both of these are surface effects, which can include variation in light and dark values and reflectance. The skin surface can appear textured because of freckles or a small quantity of hair.

With regard to textural effects the eye does not view individual shapes or motifs, but instead it sees units so small and close together that they are hard to distinguish individually and appear to fill the space. Often the surface contains a large number of tiny shapes, lines, or colors that appear to be milling about. It seems to contain a visual energy. The effect is often one of thickness or depth of surface (refer to section on indeterminate surfaces, chap. 3, for discussion). Textural effects can also

occur from an actual dense pile such as fur. A thick pile on a surface may even create its own surface (fig. 6.26).

SPATIAL POSITION. The spatial position of textured surfaces can vary in apparent distance from the viewer (fig. 6.27). The surface that has vague detail can appear to be a distance from the viewer. In actual distance viewing, the impression is similar—detail appears vague. If the textured surface contains separated colors and distinct detail of tiny individual points, it can appear closer. Such a textured surface is often defined by edge. Terms used to identify surface effects are variegated, heavy, thick, rich, shadowy, grained.

Distance of the viewer from the ABC affects the appearance of texture (fig. 6.28). Seen at close range a surface may contain a complex, allover pattern of flowers, animals, or other shapes intricately detailed and tiny. From a distance the observer may perceive a generalized, vague impression of indeterminacy.

a   b

6.27. Textured surfaces affect apparent spatial position with relation to the viewer. **a.** *Designed by Yvonne Karlsson. Used by permission.* **b.** *Photo courtesy of Fairchild Visuals, division of Fairchild Publications, Inc., New York City.*

a

6.28. Surfaces that have distinct detail appear closer to the viewer. **a.** *Photo courtesy of Joseph Gazzuolo.* **b.** *Photo courtesy of Designs by Robert Stock; photograph by Rudy Molecek.*

b

IN COMBINATION. Surfaces can contrast in texture; a rough surface placed next to a shiny one will call attention to their differences. Two surfaces combined that are similar except for texture will produce a soft and subtle, sometimes undefinable, edge.

PRIORITY OF TEXTURED SURFACES. How much a surface is noticed because of texture depends upon the viewer's impression of whether it is filled or empty (fig. 6.29). When it appears filled, surface dominates our viewing, sometimes taking priority over linear definition. The surface becomes indeterminate in character. It can also appear empty when a smooth matte surface is seemingly devoid of textural variation. This type of surface is immediately viewed and is determinate in character. Then the viewer's priority may become edge. Sometimes a determinate surface is the result of color, for example, a smooth texture accompanied by an intense primary color. When a seemingly empty surface is middle value, it is a good visual carrier of layout and light and shadow. Surface variation is somewhat masked by black, unless it can reflect light.

Color

VISUAL FUNCTION. Color can define the surface of the ABC in several different ways. Color can offer figure and focus or ground. This factor has great importance for the viewer of the ABC

6.29. At the same distance from the viewer, surfaces with a pronounced texture can occupy attention as a surface, while in those with diminished texture edge becomes a priority. *Photo courtesy of Donaldsons, Minneapolis, Minnesota.*

because the body has preexisting colors that will be influenced by other colors placed upon it. Three dimensions of color can be used to create coherence and integration or segregation of the surfaces. If any one aspect—hue, value, or intensity—of a combination of colored surfaces is similar, the colors will appear to have some visual relationship, even with the other two varying.

GENERAL APPEARANCE. Color is perceived as a surface effect of the ABC, although the ABC can be greatly influenced by colors of the surrounding areas and by lighting. Color combinations of the ABC include the body colors and those combinations of surface placed upon the body. The body colors do affect the surfaces placed upon the body and the reverse is also true.

Color has three basic dimensions that can be distinguished—hue, intensity, and value. Even though the three dimensions are combined into one viewing experience, their separation is very useful to an understanding of the effect of color. Visual relations that create grouping or segregation can be achieved by similarities or differences in any one of the three dimensions.

HUE. The name of the color as designated on the color wheel is its hue—the visual sensation of red, for example. This sensation can derive from pigments, which are chemical substances reflecting light rays, or from light rays themselves. Color related to the ABC is affected by both.

Each hue has an individual physical character: the primary hues are red, yellow, and blue; the secondary, orange, green, and violet. The secondary hues are mixtures of the adjacent primary hues; thus, orange is a mixture of red and yellow, violet is a mixture of red and

blue. The hue spectrum runs from red at one end to violet at the other, but it is usually depicted as a circle with the primary hues separated by the secondary.

Groups or categories of colors share common effects and are often called families. Adjacent hues or analogous hues are those close to one another on the color wheel, violet, blue, and green, for example. Adjacent hues on the circle are closely related sensuously.

Contrasting color schemes include complementary, split complementary, and triads. Complementary hues are hue opposites on the color wheel, such as yellow and purple-blue, and in perception can produce an afterimage of each other (fig. 6.30, *color section*). In a split complementary scheme the color on either side of the complement is selected. A triad scheme is based on hues equidistant from one another on the color wheel, such as red, yellow-green, and blue.

VALUE. The lightness-darkness dimension of a color is expressed as value. Tint is an expression of hue plus white; shade is a hue plus black. In combination, surfaces contrasting in value can affect perception of edge in the ABC. A light-value surface placed next to a dark one offers a strong visual pull to the difference between the two surfaces. An application to the ABC is the value contrast between light skin and dark hair or white shirt and black trousers or skirt (fig. 6.31). Conversely, two adjacent surfaces of similar value will create soft edges. Compare the same ABC in figure 6.30 with that in 5.17a. When value is the only dimension used, as in figure 5.17a, the visual effect of edge at center front softens.

Value without hue can be seen in gradations of gray, from white through black. The order is pictured not as a circle but as a straight line. Each hue has a normal value. The normal value for the different hues varies from lighter to darker, yellow normally being close to white or light gray and blue and violet being as dark as very dark gray. The saturated values of the complements red and green are similar, offering hue contrast but less value contrast. However, the complementary hues of yellow and blue at normal value also offer value contrast.

INTENSITY. The relative purity or saturation of a color is its intensity. Saturated colors are the primary and secondary hues at their purest on the color wheel, without any dilution by their complement. Addition of a complementary color to a hue lowers saturation toward a neutral gray. A saturated hue is intense and usually evokes a response of excitement. The less saturated colors are more neutralized and muted. Their effect is usually considered more subtle and restful. The effect of complementary colors can be subtle when less saturated (fig. 6.32, *color section*).

Intensity is perhaps the most difficult dimension of color to separate from the other two dimensions, especially when applied to body colors of the ABC. The intensity of the skin is not strong and often requires noting small differences. *Undertone* is a term used to describe underlying skin intensity and hue. Identifying skin undertone helps in placing colors on the body that are related by similarity or contrast.

WARM AND COOL. Apparent temperature is another characteristic of color relationships. Reds, yellows, and oranges are sensed as warm colors, blues and blue-greens as cool. Color warmth may be due to the association with sunshine and fire. Warm colors are

6.31. Value contrast can occur between hair and skin as well as in the materials of the ABC. *Photos courtesy of University of Minnesota; designed by Stephanie Hartigan.*

perceived as presenting an immediacy, nearness, density, a heavy impression. They are often associated with earth tones. Cool colors are associated with air, distant mountains, and water and may present an appearance of distance, depth, shadow, coolness, and lightness. Generally, the warm colors are considered to be yellow, yellow-orange, orange, red-orange, red, and red-violet. The cool colors are yellow-green, green, blue-green, blue, blue-violet, and violet. Generally, the warm hues become focus color and the cool hues become background in perception.

IN COMBINATION

SIMULTANEOUS CONTRAST. The influence of colors used in combination and in proximity to one another is referred to as simultaneous contrast. When colors are viewed at the same time, their differences in hue, value, and saturation are emphasized. Thus, colors in association with other colors can appear quite different from how they appear alone. Each color influences the neighbor to the extent that two colors can appear similar or one hue may appear as two in combination with two different colors.

Even when colors are viewed individually, color associations can affect our viewing. Hues viewed singly can produce an afterimage. After viewing an individual color for a time, the viewer sees traces of its complementary or opposite hue in what is viewed immediately after. For example, when the viewer concentrates on a costume surface and then glances at the face, the skin can appear to take on tinges of the complement to the costume's hue. Thus after looking at a green sweater, a viewer glances up at the face and it appears to contain some tinge of the complement, red.

Whether a hue is immediately surrounded by another hue or is separated in some way affects perception. For example, when individual colors are separated by black or white, both their singleness of character and their interaction are suppressed somewhat. Black causes adjacent hues to seem lighter and more brilliant; a surround of white often appears to darken them.

COLOR MIXING. Colors combined in very small patterns or woven together appear to mix visually. A color vibrancy can occur when two or more colors are interwoven into one surface. Complementary hues or black and white threads woven together will create a surface that appears gray when viewed from a distance. The visual mix will make the surface appear gray, but the gray will be more vibrant than a gray created by using all the same color gray threads. If the size of the black and white threads is increased, a salt-and-pepper effect is created. As the size of the areas of value increases and they appear more clearly and distinctly, the surface takes on the more definite values of black and gray.

SPATIAL POSITION. Color is a major definer of spatial position of a surface. Colors can appear to be near or farther away. A warm, intense yellow will seem near, while a muted, subtle gold will seem farther away. Warm colors advance and cool colors seem to retreat. An intense hue will appear closer than a less intense one. When colors dissimilar in hue, value, or intensity are combined in a pattern, their differences will often cause visual separation, attracting our attention and directing the eye (fig. 6.33, *color section*).

COLOR AS A SOURCE OF ASSOCIATED MEANING. Color is associated with many natural objects and therefore acquires similar meanings. For example, sunshine is yellow and warm: yellow is warm. Blue is cool and distant as the mountains and water. Red is exciting like fire. White is pure like the snow. Earth colors, the warm but muted hues found in the earth, suggest stability and calm.

PRIORITY OF COLOR. Surfaces can seem to be defined by color alone. When surface dominates our viewing it may be that the color is primary, intense, or by combination offers contrast of value (fig. 6.34). Color is one visual definer that, because of its ability to gain viewing attention, receives much consideration. Viewers have paid more attention to color because, perhaps more than any other visual definer, it seems the most separable. We often describe in terms of color, e.g., a red shirt, a blue dress. However, it too must be considered in the context of the ABC because the visual effect is not produced by color alone. On the body, color enters a relationship and the viewer needs to address this relationship.

Interactions of visual definers

The number of ways visual definers can be combined to create part definition is almost unlimited. One begins to wonder about ever being able to understand all of the possibilities. But a ready visual laboratory awaits — ourselves as observers. We can learn by becoming aware of how we take in the ABC and then systematically generalizing to understand the variables. We can generalize with the understanding that no specific combination of visual definers will always produce the same visual effect. The relation of a part to other parts and to the whole, its relational context, must always be considered.

6.34. Surfaces that exhibit intense contrast affect our perception of visual parts. *Photos courtesy of Designs by Robert Stock; photographs by Rudy Molecek.*

Visual exercises

I. Analyzing surface effects of an ABC.
  A. Take a large photo of an ABC. Cut a 1-inch opening in a cardboard to focus through and then describe random sections of the ABC as you move the cardboard around on the photo.
  B. Select one small area of a surface of an actual (live) ABC and watch what happens to it in motion.
  C.
    1. Examine a surface (e.g., that of a raincoat). Watch it under different conditions (e.g., in light, in shadow, in movement).
    2. Now select another surface for examination (e.g., that of a silk blouse). Watch it under similar conditions.
    3. Record observations. What differences occur?

II. Understanding the color characteristics—hue, value, and intensity.
  A. Discuss how to recognize hue, value, and intensity relations. Select examples of ABCs varying in priority of hue, value, and intensity (e.g., an ABC where value is important to visual effect).
  B. Analyze and describe colors of ABCs. Discuss size of color areas, what is figure and ground, and planar integration or separation.[1]
  C. Select an ABC for analysis. Describe color uses in the entire ABC (including body colors).
  D. Using the layout of the ABC in C, create another color scheme but use your own body colors. Repeat the body colors in the colors of the materials placed upon the body. Describe the result of similarity in hue, value, and/or intensity of body and clothing colors.

III. Analyzing the ABC for influence of color effects.
  A. Select two ABCs whose visual effect is different because of use of color (e.g., similar hues used but different value; similar hue, value, and intensity but different in use in the ABC [sizes of parts, integration of figure-ground]; different uses of hue such as complementary and analogous).
  B. Explain how the two ABCs differ in uses of color.

  Perform A and B for contrasting uses of line, shape, point, texture.

IV. Changing shapes of the ABC and relating shapes to visual effects.
  For various reasons a fashion designer, photographer, advertising artist, or window display artist may need to make substitutions that result in a change in the basic shapes of an ABC. The purpose of this exercise is to help you develop a greater awareness and therefore greater control of the impact that changing one part has on the whole. To make the exercise clear, try to consider extreme opposites in making a change.
  A. Select several full-length photographs of ABCs and number them.
  B. Using a separate piece of paper for each ABC, trace or sketch its major shapes, abstracting them into simple geometric shapes. Note their relationships.
  C. In each ABC, pick one shape, modify it through size or change of shape, and imagine the opposite or reversal (e.g., turn a triangle, substitute a circle for a square). Roughly sketch and imagine in detail a new ABC incorporating this reversal of shape.
  D. What effect does changing one part have on the whole? Has the ABC's visual effect changed? Has the figure-ground relation changed? Has the part-to-whole relation changed?
  E. Make notes on your responses and write a summary.

  Try the previous exercise isolating the color (hue, value, or intensity) or texture of one shape and reversing it, sketching and noting changes.

V. Effect of texture on the ABC.
  A. Find an example of an ABC whose visual effect you believe is mostly caused by texture.
  B. Account for the influence of texture on the ABC by examining (1) the visual order (what you see first, second, third, fourth), (2) the effect of texture on the visual order.

---

1. *The Munsell Book of Color, Neighboring Hues Edition,* is helpful in describing colors and recognizing hue, value, and intensity as separate factors.

7

Part-to-whole relations

TO understand how the ABC is organized requires responding to its visual parts, analyzing how each part is defined and related to the whole. To organize the ABC the observer is actively involved in a process of relating the part to other parts and the part to the whole.

To fully understand the function of a part in the whole requires taking into account all the basic visual parts, regardless of their visual primacy. Visual parts are units that have a measure of separation or distinction from their surround. Thus, a part in some way both separates from and defines the whole.

How the visual part functions in the whole is dependent upon its context and upon its visual definition within this context. In other words a visual part is affected not only by its own makeup but by what surrounds it. Thus, any discussion of visual part requires consideration of context. Context includes not only what is directly perceived in the visual field but also what we expect to see based upon our past experiences.

The visual part can define and integrate within the space of the ABC or define and divide the space. The part that is intimately coordinated with the whole is described as blending, and its function is that of integration within the whole. The part can also be related to the whole through contrast, becoming a source of focus in the ABC. A contrasting part is viewed as a more independent unit. While we can experience visual parts based upon their similarity to other parts, often what we first notice is the part that acts as focus, the one that offers contrast. Whether a part functions to blend or contrast within the whole is dependent upon the viewing processes of grouping and segregating.

The observer and the part

Viewing the ABC involves both grouping and segregating of visual parts. These two processes occur automatically for the observer and are going on at the same time; that is, the act of grouping requires the process of separating or detaching. What we set off for viewing is significant to the ensuing perceptual process, affecting whether we see the part or the whole first.

The observer organizes parts to give them a place in the whole: He groups when there is similarity in shape, color, size, location, direction. He segregates when visual definition involves difference and contrast or when one part is more distinct visually than another. To understand grouping and segregating of visual parts, we will refer to the Gestalt organizing factors, which are similarity, closure, proximity, and continuation (fig. 7.1).

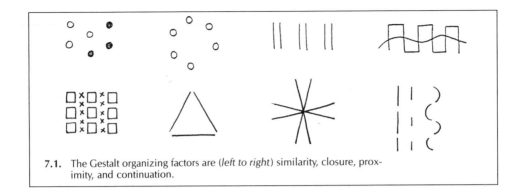

7.1. The Gestalt organizing factors are (*left to right*) similarity, closure, proximity, and continuation.

Organizing factors

SIMILARITY. Similarity is the most inclusive organizing factor and refers to the relative degree of sameness among visual parts (fig. 7.2). The perceptual connection is determined by similarity in such definers as line, shape, hue, value, texture, as well as those modifiers of the part—size, direction, weight, location. Parts that are similar in one or more aspects tend to be organized into groups by the observer and appear to lie on the same level or plane in space, that is, they become figure together. Parts that are dissimilar tend to separate from the whole.

Similar, as pertaining to parts in the whole, does not mean identical. Even parts that treat the left and right sides of the body as a mirror image are not identical. Five buttons that are identical before use in the ABC are spaced equidistant from each other down the center front. The buttons in this context are not identical because they all have a different position.

In the ABC parts can be alike or unlike in many ways. One way to see this phenomenon is to vary them in terms of definition. The same definer can appear different in differing contexts in the ABC. For example, the same blue color may reflect differently from two surfaces varying in visual texture. A circle repeated throughout the ABC can gradually become less distinct in outline. A part can

7.2. Parts similar in shape, color, texture, line may group in perception. **a.** *Photo courtesy of University of Minnesota, Goldstein Gallery; photographer, Judy Olausen.* **b.** and **c.** *Photos courtesy of University of Minnesota, Goldstein Gallery; photographer, Michelle Madson.*

a

b

c

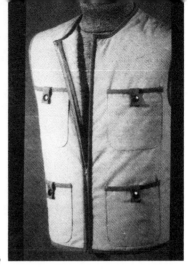

7.3. Lines and shapes may be perceived as closed even if they are not. **a.** *Photo courtesy of University of Minnesota, Goldstein Gallery; photographer, Michelle Madson.* **b.** *Photo courtesy of University of Minnesota.*

be similar to another in hue but lighter in value. A second way to illustrate the many similarities of ABC parts is to vary them by combination with other definers: lines, shapes, textures, and colors. A circle and a triangle shape can both be blue. In the ABC this could be the triangle of a tie or handkerchief and the circle of a pin or a surface print.

When visual parts in the ABC become complex, they may relate in several or even many different ways within the whole. For example, a part may be similar in size to one part and similar in color to another part. The observer may connect the part first with the part similar in size and then with the one similar in color. Most likely the degree of connection will influence the organizing process, that is, if two parts are similar in both size and color, the clearest, least ambiguous organization would be perceived first.

Parts that are not similar are viewed as segregated or separate and are often sources of focus. While we experience the wholeness of visual forms based upon similarity, what we focus upon may be the part that is dissimilar or a change from the expected. This contrast can originate from the visual definition of the ABC or from the observer's associated ideas. It is significant what first segregates as a part. (Refer to chap. 8 for discussion of function of parts.)

CLOSURE. Closure refers to the perception of detachment or separation of a visual part. Lines and shapes that are nearly complete are readily perceived as complete or closed. This concept of closure implies viewer participation in filling in the blanks (fig. 7.3). Line can be implied by the viewer and thus does not actually need to be connected to be perceived so. Often, when a visual part is not entirely closed or bounded, the observer will fill in the outline if it provides a clearer meaning. The observer who fills in to close may group buttons to create a rectangle or even connect the lines created by pockets and buttons or buttons and collar.

Visual perception is a process of scanning and then focusing. We focus on manageable portions of our visual field at any one time. Thus, we must first close to separate what we want to view, then focus upon what we have closed off. As discussed in chapter 3, the whole ABC or a part may separate first.

The process of closure can involve grouping as well as segregating. What has the most contrast and the greatest detachment from the surround will create the strongest closure. This detachment can be as large as the entire silhouette of the ABC or as small as a button. If we are looking at the ABC in its entirety, a sharply defined silhouette will become a frame of reference in our viewing, especially if no other part is as sharply defined. If the silhouette is not as dominant visually as is a button or group of buttons, they may take priority in the viewing process.

PROXIMITY. Parts that are close together will group in perception. Proximity is similarity of location or close spatial placement. As the distance between similar parts varies, those that are close spatially will tend to group as might two rows of stitching on a pocket (fig. 7.4). The observer is less likely to group two parts that are far apart.

Given the complexity of the ABC, grouping of physically close visual units may occur when only one aspect of the units is similar, e.g., hair and neck scarf with similar color but different shape and size. This occurs especially when the parts are in close proximity and surrounded by seemingly open space.

Proximity also means similarity of location in apparent distance from the observer. Thus two similar determinate surfaces will appear to lie a similar distance from the viewer and will group on one level. An indeterminate and a determinate surface will tend to separate as parts since they will appear to be different distances from the viewer.

Parts can be spatially close in a number of ways in the ABC. Two parts can touch boundaries, overlap, or be detached but close together. When two or more parts overlap, the part that covers the other may appear to be on top. When the two parts are transparent, there may be a visual penetration of one part by another or the formation of a new part where the two parts coincide.

Each part relationship can produce different spatial effects. When two parts are detached but close or touching, they may appear equidistant from the viewer or one may appear closer and one farther away. How the surface is defined influences the spatial effect. In overlapping, the part that has a continuous

7.4. Parts close together group in perception. Lines and shapes create grouping and segregating of parts. *Photos courtesy of University of Minnesota, Goldstein Gallery; photographer, Michelle Madson.*

 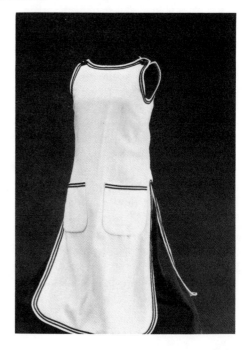

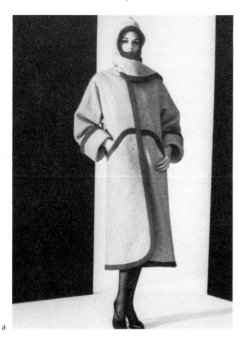

7.5. **a.** Parts with continuous contour tend to group. *Photo courtesy of Minneapolis College of Art and Design; designed by Sharon Wendel.* **b.** Zigzag lines of the cape may be viewed as continuing but the black at center front also continues from head to toe. *Photo courtesy of Minneapolis College of Art and Design; designed by Regina Simmons Tarver.*

boundary usually appears on top or above the other. If neither part appears on top, which may occur with transparent fabrics, the parts may become a combined and a new part.

CONTINUATION. Parts arranged in a straight or curvilinear path result in perception of grouping. Continuation is that connecting of parts in perception that occurs because parts follow a direction (fig. 7.5). Examples are the center front pleat of a skirt that continues a line of buttons in a jacket or a long string of beads that continues the visual path of a line of dangling earrings.

Lines and shapes with more connecting and continuous contours tend to be more definite configurations than those with discontinuous contours. A discontinuous contour occurs when there is an abrupt change in direction, which tends to create separate visual parts. A skirt hem by changing the vertical line of the leg to the horizontal edge of the skirt shape causes the skirt to be viewed as a separate visual part. A point of focus often occurs at the place in the line where a contour changes direction.

Context can aid continuation. If the continuation of form is reinforced by a similar meaning the grouping is stronger (fig. 7.6). A series of horizontal stripes placed in a vertical shape on the body could be viewed as a continuous vertical path. Also the reverse is true, i.e., if a discontinuous outline is reinforced by a change in meaning it will be more strongly segregated. For example, a jacket edge that changes direction from silhouette to hem edge (vertical to horizontal) is still perceived more strongly

7.6. The viewer may continue a line from dissimilar parts such as a lapel and row of buttons, as well as similar parts such as pockets.

than the continuous edge of the silhouette of jacket and trousers.

Thus, relatively dissimilar parts can be grouped by continuation. In a row of buttons, if one button was unbuttoned, it would be easier to perceive the buttons as a continuous grouping if the one unbuttoned was in the middle of the row. Then the eye would be less likely to stop.

INTERACTION. The Gestalt organizing factors occur together in the organizing process. Organizing is the process of combining and relating the visual parts. Thus visual parts that are similar, closed, in close proximity, and continuous will group, and those that are not will separate as parts. The stability of the relationships depends upon their clarity, their lack of ambiguity. When the four organizing factors compete in a visual form, the most clear and stable solution is the one that will prevail for the viewer (fig. 7.7).

Part modifiers

A visual part is affected not only by its own makeup but by what surrounds it. Context of a visual part includes not only what is directly sensed in the visual field, the visual definers, but also how we compare the part to other parts and to the whole. The interaction of visual parts in the whole is influenced by such modifiers as number, size, location on the body, and position in space.

NUMBER. The significance of a visual part changes with number. A single, isolated unit is perceived differently as a visual part than a quantity of the same unit is. According to Krome Barratt in his book *Logic and Design,* the number of similar visual units a viewer can take in without counting or grouping is around seven. The number any viewer can take in without counting is called a number threshold. When we are confronted with one to seven items, we can easily assess the number and respond with an awareness of their separateness. However, when we see more than seven, we must begin to group in order to respond. In the case of the eight buttons in figure 7.6 the viewer may group into two rows of four or four rows of two.

Past a threshold of seven or so, we must group or order the parts to compre-

7.7. The viewer should be able to perceive examples of at least two organizing factors in each jacket. Does one prevail?

hend number. For example, twelve units may be grouped into four rows of three units each. The viewer may perceive up to seven groups. Past seven groups of seven, we begin to experience numerical dazzle until the groups of units evolve into pattern.

Pattern is experienced as an ordered repetition of shapes on a surface. Pattern usually involves a grouping process and a conscious repetition. A pattern is assisted by easily comprehensible repeats or grouping of groups.

The groupings on the body involve an order and one grouping can become more important than another in manner of use. Think of how one group of dots, for example, can become more important than another when used on the body. By gathering a surface imprinted with groups of dots, the dots lose their separateness. The gathers may supersede the dots and take on visual priority. If a portion of the same surface is placed flat on the body, and often this is done in the upper torso, then that area may gain dominance in viewing, and an order has been introduced.

As we group like shapes or lines they can become more important in several respects. Five buttons can be perceived as an enclosed shape or as a line with direction or continuation. When working with two mirror image shapes, we can experience a hierarchy by placing a handkerchief in the pocket on one side of the jacket or a pin on one lapel. This asymmetrical treatment makes the side treated with a handkerchief or pin visually more important. If both sides were treated similarly, for example, with shoulder epaulets, then one side is not more important or dominant. Symmetry has prevailed.

Within the understanding of the concept of number is that of unit and interval. When two parts or units are perceived as a group of two, an interval is

7.8. Stripes are perceived as figure because of the unit and interval of the stripes. *Photo courtesy of University of Minnesota, Goldstein Gallery; photographer, Michelle Madson.*

required between them. If this interval is fairly explicit, the two units become grouped as figure (fig. 7.8). If no interval is experienced, the two become one part. If the two units are moved a greater distance from each other, the space between may not be perceived as an interval but as another unit.

DIRECTION. The viewer is usually involved in perceiving a number of visual parts. Direction refers to the experience of movement while taking in the ABC. This occurs because seeing takes time. The impression of movement is largely temporal since it occurs in the mind while the viewer is experiencing the form. The viewer is involved in a process of scan, focus, scan, focus and is thus led throughout the ABC. How a part is experienced, in the focus or the scanning process, influences its place in the whole. Focus is an arrest; scanning is moving from one visual unit to another.

Movement within the ABC involves the direction the visual parts take in rela-

7.9. Lines and shapes on the body direct the viewer. *Photo courtesy of University of Minnesota, Goldstein Gallery; photographer, Michelle Madson.*

7.10. Diagonal lines depart from the vertical of the body axis. *Photo courtesy of Fairchild Visuals, division of Fairchild Publications, Inc., New York City.*

tion to the basic axis of the ABC (fig. 7.7). A line or shape on the body expresses some direction, either related to the vertical-horizontal axes of the body or departing from them (fig. 7.9). A vertical line often reinforces the vertical axis. A diagonal line, which opposes the body axis, depending upon its relation to the entire shape of the ABC, may be experienced as having more energy than a vertical line (fig. 7.10). A shape such as a rectangle, by itself, has a direction, i.e., length is greater than width and directs the eye. When placed on the body the long way, it reinforces the body verticality. If placed horizontally on the body, it may reinforce the basic vertical-horizontal axes. It may also create parts on the body, depending upon other factors such as number or clarity, in other words, its contextual relation.

Visual parts may involve more than one direction within the ABC. In addition to planar direction, or horizontal-vertical, parts can also exhibit in-out movement from the surface of the ABC, creating an impression of depth.

Direction can be aided by repetition of similar parts, often called rhythm. Rhythm is defined as the ordered reoccurrence of parts. It makes use of an observer's expectations of regular repetition of, for example, pleats in a shirt or beads in a necklace.

Rhythm is never an exact repetition of the same part in the ABC. The identical part repeated on the body is never the same because it cannot occupy the same space. As discussed under Similarity, three buttons may be identical before placement in the ABC, but once in context, the buttons are not identical. Their position varies, one being in the middle of the other two, and so forth.

The repetition that occurs in patterns printed on surfaces can be interrupted with draping into folds and through body contours and body movements. Even though the pleats encircling the body are not totally repetitious, for they occur differently on the various planes of the body and in different body views, they may group by similarity. The eye may see the continuous line made by the row of pleats or beads rather than the pleats or beads themselves.

When the unit and interval are perceived as two parts, we scan alternately between them. This occurs when the eye is led from a black to a white stripe placed vertically on the body or from the highlight of the top of a pleat to the shadow of the recess. Often some variation in visual part gives the eye something to take in more separately, thus directing the eye to move from one part to the next.

Another type of directing occurs because of gradation, which is a measured change from one part to another. The viewer experiences a progression from one part to the next because of a change in the parts. For example, a color may change in value gradually from dark to light or a shape may progress in size from large to small (fig. 7.11).

Direction is often experienced in the ABC because the body structure involves gradation, such as from larger limbs of the lower body to smaller limbs of the upper body. In a body suit conforming to the body curves, the gradation is obvious. The body may also produce a gradation with items put on it, for example, crisp pleats that vary in width or soft folds of a fabric varying in depth and in play of light and shadow because of interaction with the body structure.

SIZE. Parts may vary in size in relation to one another and they are compared for similarities and differences. Similar size is one factor in grouping (fig. 7.12). In the ABC the sizes of parts are also compared to the size of the body (fig. 7.13).

7.11. Gradation from wider to narrower directs the eye. *Photo courtesy of University of Minnesota, Goldstein Gallery; photographer, Judy Olausen.*

7.12. Parts similar in size tend to group. Parts different in size segregate. *Photo courtesy of University of Minnesota; photographer, Leo Perry.*

7.13. Size and location of shapes on the body affect perception of parts. *Photo courtesy of Chou Chou, St. Paul, Minnesota.*

Proportion refers to the size relations of the parts to each other and to the whole. The size of a shape enters into a proportional relation when it is read in the context of other shapes. However, the apparent size of the shape is influenced by surface color and texture.

What we judge as proportional with regard to the ABC changes with time. Absolute rules have been developed through actual physical measurement for what is considered a "good" proportional experience. But in viewing an ABC we cannot stop to take precise measurements. What we can conclude from such rules is that unequal sizes are more interesting than equal ones. With unequal proportions we must consider the parts in relation to each other and to the whole. If one part is much larger than others, it may segregate and not appear related at all. If the larger part is perceived as clearly dominant, it can become a focus within the ABC.

If the ABC is taken in as a whole first, we make proportional judgments based upon that reference. The key to making judgments is to be aware of the conventional and timely relationships and to make them from that reference. For example, when the fit of clothing becomes larger and looser, its relation to the body changes in our view of the ABC. This changed relation may require an increase in the size of all the ABC parts in order to be proportional. When the size of the lapels of a suit change in width, we change our judgments of proportion accordingly.

One proportional reference viewers always have is their own body. As we grow taller as a society, our concept of tall changes. We compare our own body height to that of others. Models of the ABC in illustration or photography are often 9–l0 heads in height. While this proportion has been useful for the proper hang and drape of fabrics on the body, it exceeds the average. Viewing this proportion in fashion images surely can affect our expectations of our own bodies and our frame of reference for ABC proportion.

Manipulating the visual definers can create different proportional relationships. Changing the size of a repeat motif can change its appearance and place in the whole. A large shape will appear closer, while a small shape will seem farther away, other things being equal (fig. 7.14). But a small shape contrasting with the surround will often become focus. Degree of surface definition influences whether a shape will appear to advance or recede.

VISUAL WEIGHT. In the process of viewing the ABC we are continuously involved in comparing one part with another. This comparison involves an unconscious visual weighting because of surface texture, size of shape, and the like. A surface that appears dense and filled may be weighted more than one that appears empty. When one part is experienced as weighing more than another, a hierarchy is established. When one part is experienced as approximately equal to another, we perceive a balance.

Visual interest operates as if it possessed weight. Even though all parts of the ABC exist at an equal distance from the observer, some appear to come forward and some recede. A part that appears to advance because of a larger size or a more intense color gains more attention. Balance by interest is achieved by varying the amount of attention of the visual parts.

The easiest way to achieve equal weighting, or balance, in the ABC is through bilateral symmetry, a situation of identical left and right halves of the visual field. This type of symmetrical balance is very easy for the observer to take

7.14. The observer groups the stripes similar in size and views the wider stripes before the narrower ones. *Photo courtesy of University of Minnesota; designed by Georgia Scheu.*

in; it requires a minimum of effort, especially when body symmetry is repeated in the clothing. However, there are many other possibilities in visual weighting.

The concept of a balanced ABC is based on its apparent visual weight. Balance includes both weighting in terms of the plane parallel to the observer, left-right, top-bottom visual weight, and the experience of in-out or near-far, from the observer, the apparent distance of the visual parts (fig. 7.15).

A grouping of parts (those similar in color, texture, size, shape, location) will often appear heavier than a single part.

Visually we compare the parts of an ABC and weigh them against others.

Where a part is located on the body affects its visual weight. The body provides a hierarchy for viewing and the viewer tends to give more attention to the upper portion of the ABC. A grouping of parts may combine adjacent body parts, for example, the head and upper torso, or create a directing movement because the eye groups nonadjacent parts, for example, similar color hair and skirt.

Dissimilar parts are viewed in comparison to each other. For example, a coarsely textured surface will appear to

a b c

7.15. Parts are visually compared as they relate to each other and to the ABC. **a.** *Photo courtesy of Joseph Gazzuolo.* **b.** *Photo courtesy of Fairchild Visuals, division of Fairchild Publications, Inc., New York City.* **c.** *Photo courtesy of University of Minnesota, Goldstein Gallery; photographer, Judy Olausen.*

be heavier by comparison with a smooth one. The contrast between the two is what is noticed and each surface affects the experience of the other. Balance by contrast is a type of asymmetrical balance that requires a comparison of the visual demands of two or more parts.

In perceiving the body we may experience weighting of the upper-lower body treatment as balanced or unbalanced, i.e., as an equality or a dominance. Balance is a perceptual condition and depends upon the context of each ABC. If we perceive the upper portion of the body as dominant because of a strong horizontal line across the shoulders in contrast to the head size and the rest of the body, we give more attention to this line.

On the other hand, in a comparison of similar colors or patterns throughout the body, we may experience a dominance not of one body part but of the whole body. A border print placed at the shoulder area and repeated at the hem requires eye movement over more of the body. The amount of border print at the shoulder may be smaller than the amount at the hem, but shoulder position alone may create a visual equality of the two areas.

Habits of perception affect how we view a visual form and treatments of the ABC take this factor into consideration. In English, we read from left to right. Often the left side of the ABC is balanced with the right with this left-right viewing order in mind. An interesting detail on the left can lead the eye into the rest of the ABC.

Balance can also refer to the physical position of the ABC we are viewing. If that body appears off balance temporarily, as though it would not stay in its current position for long, the observer feels a tension.

SPATIAL POSITION

LEVELS OF PARTS IN THE WHOLE. An observer needs to consider how parts group—on one level or several? If visual parts are similar, they group on one level, or plane, above the surface, as figure on ground. Examples of this type of grouping are created by a simple surface pattern or a repeated motif or shape. Of-

7.16. Shapes that contrast as figure against ground appear closer than shapes that are more integrated with ground. *Photos courtesy of University of Minnesota; photographer, Leo Perry.*

ten we experience similar lines or shapes as a grid slightly above the ground. Grouping on one level includes everything that appears equidistant from the observer.

Consider the apparent distance between the levels of parts that group as figure, whether the levels appear to lie close together or farther away. The grouping may appear to be quite close to, or integrated with, the ground or it may appear to separate from the ground

(fig. 7.16). When we say that a surface has a spotty effect, we usually mean that the figure appears to be closed and separated and a considerable distance from the ground.

The figure-ground relation may be quite clear cut and unambiguous for the viewer, that is, the figure always appears to lie in a spatial position above the ground. However, ambiguity in spatial position can occur. Competition between figure and ground can provide an

7.17. Competition between figure and ground can create tension for the viewer. *Photo courtesy of University of Minnesota; photographer, Leo Perry.*

energy and tension (fig. 7.17). Then the viewer is able to reverse the figure and ground. What at first appears as figure can become ground in an ambiguous figure-ground relation. Figure-ground ambiguity can be controlled. When a surface is ambiguous as to figure-ground, visual cues are often introduced that reduce ambiguity. In certain situations ambiguity lends interest. Some designers have experimented with figure-ground ambiguity, especially for evening. Photographers often use figure-ground ambiguity to create interest.

Grouping on more than one level, or plane, can be applied to the layout of visual parts of the ABC. As organization occurs there may be distinct levels of two-dimensional or three-dimensional surfaces. When surfaces of the ABC become three-dimensional through use, they may gradually curve in and out. For example, if a piece of lace is viewed flat, it is seen mainly as a linear tracery in two dimensions. But lace worn as a veil or trimming may appear as lines or as flexible shapes. It is constantly moving and may fall into soft folds on the body. The openings may reveal additional layers underneath, of skin or another fabric. Here grouping on distinct levels does not occur and the surface appears indeterminate.

In the ABC, indeterminate surfaces appear thicker due to indefinite shape, texture, or shadow and light playing on the surface. Often the indeterminate surface appears farther away from the observer and this factor is used by the viewer in ordering by levels (fig 7.18). A determinate surface is clearly defined and definite in its relation to the observer. It is relatively free of three-dimensional light-and-shadow effects and often has sharp edges. There is little doubt as to where and how a determinate surface occurs in space.

APPARENT DISTANCE. Our judgment of an object's distance is affected by our early experience in giving meaning to what we see. By the time we are adults the means by which we estimate distance are quite unconscious. However, making them conscious will help in understanding the part-to-whole relation in the ABC.

Normally our assessment of distance is approximate and simplified to near-far. Within the viewer's personal space, distance is judged precisely and objects usually appear clear. From a distance they can appear blurred (fig. 7.19). The size of this personal space varies with activity and expectations. Past this space, we are concerned mostly with similarity and comparisons of more than and less than.

There are a number of attributes of shapes in space that cause the shapes to appear in certain positions as they relate to each other. For example, a large circle will appear closer to the viewer than a smaller one does, given that other as-

7.18. Surfaces varying in degree of indeterminacy provide levels and an order for the viewer. *Photo courtesy of Giorgio Armani; photographer, Aldo Fallai.*

7.19. Shapes can appear to be closer to or farther away from the viewer. *Photos courtesy of Joseph Gazzuolo.*

pects such as color and texture remain equal. A sharp edge is experienced as more immediate and a blurred edge is farther away. The apparent spatial distance of attributes is directly related to our past experiences with identifying the relation of both things and people in space to ourselves (fig. 7.20).

7.20. Past experiences in viewing distance based on size and on degree of distinctness and clarity affect our spatial organization of visual forms. **a., b.,** and **c.** *Photos courtesy of Joseph Gazzuolo; his students' work (a) Random Marks, (b) Grid Study.* **d.** *Photo courtesy of Robert Hillestad; Garden Study I (detail).*

We need to think about what characteristics of an object make it appear to be a given distance from us. As shown in the example of a large and a smaller circle, size is a factor in distance viewing. Several objects of the same size, shape, and color will appear to lie on the same plane. A greater difference in size creates a greater difference in apparent spatial position (fig. 7.21). If a large star is accompanied by a somewhat smaller star in our visual field, we organize them on similar planar levels. However, if the large star is accompanied by some very much smaller stars, the viewer begins to consider unlimited space, being unable to judge how far away the stars are from each other.

When viewing patterned surfaces, one begins to realize their potential variety. Patterns can appear as allover texture when shapes are not self-contained and do not appear in a distinct figure-ground relation. Patterns with repeated but more individual shapes can be viewed in a distinct figure-ground relation (figs. 7.22, 7.23). If they are similar in size, the shapes will appear to lie an equal distance from the ground, given equality of other factors. We group the shapes with each other and at the same time we segregate or separate them from the ground.

The same process occurs with different sizes and shapes when we consider the layout of the ABC. We group what is similar and separate what is different. Thus, we can view the ABC as having a finite number of levels or, if there are too many different sizes and shapes, infinity. After a certain number we do not continue to group; we simply note degree of indeterminacy.

Apparent distance can be applied to other visual definers, such as color, cool colors appearing to retreat and warm colors to advance. If a blue shape is placed adjacent to and surrounding a yellow

7.21. The greater the difference in size between shapes, the greater the apparent distance between surfaces. *Photo courtesy of University of Minnesota; photographer, Leo Perry.*

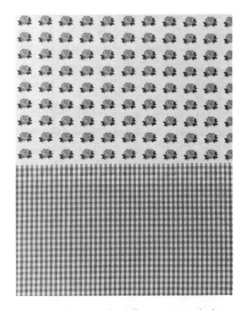

7.22. Patterns can be allover repeated shapes creating a grid above the ground. *Photo courtesy of University of Minnesota; photographer, Leo Perry.*

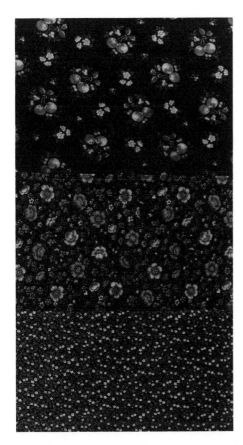

7.23. Patterns can range from small-sized to larger redundant shapes. Similar-sized shapes tend to group in perception. *Photo courtesy of University of Minnesota; photographer, Leo Perry.*

Intensity. An intense, bright hue appears closer than one less intense.

Shape. A shape that appears self-contained and enclosed appears closer than one that is open and integrated with the ground. The simplest shape to see is a circle and it usually appears to be closer than a shape with a more complex edge.

Line, Edge. A line or shape with a clear boundary appears closer than one that is not clearly outlined or is blurred. Opaque surfaces usually have more clearly defined lines and edges than do transparent surfaces.

Surface texture. Obvious or coarse microlayout appears closer than fine.

To apply these principles to the ABC, let us consider one attribute above—edge. Edges make a difference in the visual character of any object. What edges are possible in the entire ABC? There are the edges within the items of apparel themselves: a shirt has pocket and collar edges; it also may have edges derived from a surface pattern. There are edges created by the relation of the shirt perimeter to the body, as where the neckline of the shirt and the neck meet. Finally, there are edges in the relation of the ABC to the immediately surrounding space, for example, the edges created by the sleeve of the shirt and the adjoining space. All of these edges are possible, but which are viewed as closer and therefore of greater priority will depend upon how distinct each appears.

The nature of the adjoining space affects what types of edges are created. White tennis shoes, for example, would have soft edges when surrounded by snow and hard edges when surrounded by black dirt. When worn with white socks they would have a soft edge between the sock and the tennis shoe and when worn with black socks, a hard edge.

The part with its many definers and

one, the blue will look as if it lies behind the yellow, especially if the boundaries are blurred somewhat. This appearance may be due to our previous associations in viewing distance.

Some generalizations can be made concerning attributes that affect the apparent position of a visual part in space:

Hue. A warm hue appears closer than a cool hue given similar value and intensity.

Value. Surfaces contrasting in value appear closer than surfaces similar in value.

modifiers must be considered within the context of the whole ABC. Exceptions can always be found to the spatial position, or apparent distance, of a specific attribute of the ABC when it is considered as a separate visual phenomenon and not a part of the whole.

Visual exercises

I. Understanding visual part-to-whole effects in the ABC.
  A. Select at least two ABCs and explain uses made of similarity, proximity, closure, and continuation.
  B. In your ABCs, which characteristics are grouping and which are separating? Which of the organizing factors are influencing the process? Keeping in mind that the organizing factors can occur simultaneously, are any of the four competing?

II. Understanding apparent distance and spatial position in the ABC.
  A. Compare differences in visual effect between objects in your near space and in your far space.
  B. Apply these differences to yourself as an ABC as you look in a mirror. How could you dress to appear more immediate to the viewer? How could you dress to appear farther away from the viewer?
  C. If you had to design an ABC for the theater, how would you control the visual effect from a distance? Of the main actor, who must attract attention upon entering? Of a minor character who remains in the background?

III. Organization of ABC—modifying visual effect.
  The character and number of visual parts in an ABC affects perception of the whole. In this exercise you will explore the modification of visual parts. Perception of a visual part involves boundaries. A boundary can be perceived as a line and/or as a shape. For example, by placing a black 4-inch-square piece of paper next to a white 4-inch-square piece of paper, two aspects of these parts are visible. There is a boundary line that is formed between the white area and the black area, and there is the dominant shape of the white square and the black square. If a dark-value navy blue piece of fabric with a flat texture were to be placed next to a similarly textured black piece of fabric, the boundary line would become blurred, subtle to the observer, and the two surfaces might visually appear as one whole more easily than as two parts. If a shiny, dark-value navy blue piece of fabric were to be placed next to a matte black piece of fabric, the boundary line would be subtle, but the shape could be viewed as two parts, most likely with the shiny surface slightly in front.

  Definers used to achieve visual parts include line, shape, color, texture. Boundaries can range from distinct and bold in nature to soft, subtle, or ambiguous. Examples of distinct boundaries in the ABC include those created by value differences (e.g., black hair next to pale skin), by shape differences (e.g., a bulky fur jacket next to skinny pants), or by hue variations (e.g., a red snowsuit in a surround of white snow). Examples of subtle boundaries include those of textural differences (e.g., light brown hair against tanned skin), of blending colors of the same value, or of the light and shadow play of soft, blurred lines often seen in folds of fabric. The types of boundaries created affects the part-to-whole relation of the ABC.

  A. Select a sketch with explicit visual details. Keep the sketch constant throughout this exercise. Imagine and illustrate three different visual modifications that would alter the character of the visual parts. Specifically, create visual plans to achieve the following: (1) an ABC with several visual parts with subtle, soft-edged boundaries, viewed as a whole; (2) an ABC with one visual part that dominates the visual plan; and (3) an ABC with several visual parts, which are viewed first as parts, with bold, hard edges between them. Include the entire ABC in your three modifications. This means physical coloring, accessories, and so forth.
  B. Write a paragraph explaining (1) how the differences in visual effect were achieved (e.g., through the use of colors, textures, light and shadow) and (2) how the character of the visual part affected the perception of the whole (what is viewed first, second, etc.).

8

Interpreting the ABC: form organization

THOSE factors of analysis that define and modify the visual part have been discussed. The part can be defined by line, shape, point, color, and texture; it can be related to the whole ABC by modifiers and the Gestalt principles of organization. Now we will see how these factors affect the visual result. To interpret the form means to consider what summarizes and explains it.

The viewer and the ABC

The organizing process is an interplay between the viewer and the form. To organize the ABC the viewer must be actively involved in taking in the form, relating various distinguishable parts to other parts and to the whole. In this process, the way the form is structured directs the viewer—where the viewer focuses first, how strong the focus, how many foci are perceived. These two factors—structure and visual relationships—influence the organizing process.

Perception is a process of scan and focus, or put another way, a combination of contextual viewing and focal viewing. The viewer can only focus on small areas of a visual field at any one time, but the context plays a role in what becomes focus. Thus, we first scan and separate what we are going to view. When we focus on a part, the remainder of the ABC becomes ground or periphery in

perception. As we continue to examine the entire ABC, the relationships within the form become evident.

Attending is both attraction and sustained viewing. Attraction is dependent upon the degree of definition and the qualities that make a form different from other forms. What first attracts attention are those contrasts in the visual field that become sources of focus and priority. For example, the silhouette of a closed ABC will play a dominant role because it will attract attention and influence the relationships of parts. If the silhouette is open and interacting with the surround, it may play a secondary role, especially if there is a more contrasting part that focuses attention.

Sustained attention is a result of the visual relations among the parts. We organize based upon the degree of similarity and difference between one part and other parts and the whole. We compare the degree of connectedness of parts within context. Visual relationships invite the comparison. The viewer remains interested by keeping active in the perceptual process.

The organizing process

The viewer perceives organization whenever possible: Similar visual parts are grouped; contrasting or different visual parts are separated. Grouping and separating occur automatically for the viewer, but to understand organizing, the viewer must become conscious of the process.

The viewer can understand the visual effect by becoming aware of the organizing process. The viewer's first task in understanding a form is to scan the whole. How much space is occupied? How is the eye directed within the form? His or her second task is to ask, What becomes focus? What is the nature of the visual relationships? Steps that aid the process are as follows:

l. Scan the whole. What attracts attention first, second, third? What is the main direction of scanning?

2. What are points of focus? How many centers of focus are there—the whole, one part, many parts?

3. Analyze the organizing process.

a. Viewing path: Is it directed within one body view? Is it directed to the body cylinder, to silhouette? Is it vertical, horizontal, diagonal?

b. Space of ABC: Does the silhouette offer closure for the viewer (closed or open)? Is the space within solid or broken up (part or whole, planar integration or segregation)? How do the surfaces appear (flat or rounded, determinate or indeterminate)?

c. The entry: What is the location and source of first focus? Is viewing arrested within one area?

d. Function of parts: What differences occur among the parts? How many are there? How are parts similar to each other and to the whole? What is their nature—contrasting and independent or blending and interdependent?

The visual result

The visual result is the cumulative effect on the viewer produced by the distinctive way in which materials are arranged within the ABC. Forms differ in their visual priorities, that is, the extent of and degree to which sudden breaks occur and the extent to which they are linked or related again. Forms differ in the amount of space they occupy and the character of that space, whether they appear to be a solid mass or to have parts that break up the space.

The form can be summarized according to the way it affects the viewer. Use of the five word pairs introduced in chapter 3 is a good beginning to this process. They can lead to an understanding of the types of spatial relationships that are primary in the ABC. Patterns will become evident, e.g., some combinations will often be together such as viewing of the whole as figure and planar integration. Whether the viewer is attracted by parts or the whole, surfaces or edges, single focus or multiple foci has much to do with the ultimate communication and meaning of that form.

The ABC is defined by particular lines, shapes, colors, and textures. How the definers are combined affects viewing. For example, if a shape is similar to one shape but different from another, the shapes begin to have different types of relationships. When shapes are equal in visual weight but not similar enough to group, they will remain more independent as parts. These parts can direct the viewer. If parts are unequal in visual weight (e.g., varying in size) they can create an order or sequence that also directs viewing.

Some ABCs are easier to view than others. Some are viewed as a whole immediately. Some have a clearly established viewing order and are read successively because each part has a place. An ABC that appears less sequential usually contains independent and more equal parts. Such a form requires more time for viewing and is more separated into parts.

a b c

8.1. ABCs viewed simultaneously as a whole. **a.** *Designed by Jhane Barnes; photographer, Jade Albert. Used by permission.* **b.** *Photo courtesy of Perry Ellis Sportswear.* **c.** *Designed by Gene Ewing. Used by permission.*

Easy viewing is not necessarily the final goal of all visual forms. Some ABCs invite a simultaneous viewing because of a blending of interdependent parts within the whole (fig. 8.1). Some have a simplicity, clarity, and precision of message, arising from a successive ordering. Such a form may have parts that are both independent and dependent within the whole (fig. 8.2). Other forms may invite

a b c

8.2. ABCs viewed in a successive manner. **a.** *Designed by Oscar de la Renta; photo by Jesse Gerstein. Used by permission.* **b.** *Designed by Jerry Silverman. Used by permission.* **c.** *Designed by Oscar de la Renta. Used by permission.*

a   b   c

8.3. ABCs viewed as separate parts. **a.** *Photo courtesy of Donaldsons, Minneapolis, Minnesota.* **b.** *Dinner dress from the Fall 1985 Collection of Morton Myles for the Warrens; designed by Morton Myles. Used by permission.* **c.** *Designs by Robert Stock; photograph by Rudy Molecek.*

attention to contrasting parts that are equal in visual weight and more independent; these forms are seemingly more random and separated because of the way the parts are viewed (fig. 8.3). Table 2 is a descriptive summary of the part-to-whole relation and the way the ABC is organized.

TABLE 2. *Categories of ABC organization*

Simultaneous	Successive	Separated
View whole first, many secondary foci	One primary focus and/or several secondary foci	Several primary foci, view parts first
Blending parts dependent upon position in whole	Some parts unequal weight and some equal	Parts equal weight, independent and contrasting

EFFECT OF PAST EXPERIENCES. As a viewer attends to an ABC, past experiences are reflected in the organizing process. The viewer carries memories of ABCs and of experiences viewing them. Patterns of viewing become established. The viewer of any one form compares that form with those seen before. A form can be very much like other forms in the viewer's experience, making it easier to view and understand. Variations of that form can be based upon prior knowledge. For example, a blazer jacket is a known layout structure. Surface structuring can override some of the layout, but the viewer continues to refer to the blazer layout as a given, describing it as a plaid blazer. Thus our past experiences influence the present experience of attending and describing what we view.

If a viewer is not experienced in the organizing process or is not aware of differences in visual effect, a comparison of two forms will often provide clues to the distinctiveness of each.

EFFECT OF PURPOSEFUL INVOLVEMENT. Attending is often related to a purpose. That purpose can be simply to establish the amount of interest a form possesses. But it can also be to relate the form to a given situation, for example, the appropriateness of the form for an event. ABCs viewed as possessing a sense of immediacy and a highly developed and expected order may be associated with a business situation. Others, viewed with a sustained attention, even a lingering in the viewing of the whole, may call to mind a gala event when there is time for intrigue and intricacy in viewing. If we are attending in order to choose what to wear, we may be concerned with the way we will look as an ABC.

Purpose can get in the way of understanding form organization and visual result. If we can first begin to understand the range of visual possibilities by getting acquainted with a variety of forms, then we can begin to draw upon this knowledge to consider purposes of situation and wearer.

CONTROLLING CONTEXTUAL FEATURES. A controlling feature is a part or part property that influences the visual result. The visual effect of an ABC is a fusion of separable definers and modifiers. The visual definers, like the separate ingredients in lemonade, can be isolated and described as properties of a part and this is an important first step. But even though the part has a particular color, texture, and shape, this does not totally characterize its relation to the whole. The properties do not exist in isolation, and how they relate to each other and the context of the particular ABC influences their visual effect.

The importance of the part in the whole has been emphasized throughout this book. Another way of saying this is: The whole is more than the sum of its parts. What happens is illustrated by the comparison to lemonade, which is a fusion of lemons, sugar, and water. Lemonade is better understood by knowing its ingredients. But knowing what each ingredient tastes like is not the same as knowing the taste of lemonade.

By itself a definer is an ingredient to describe, as in the example in figure 8.4, color values of two ABCs with the same layout structure. The ABC on the right is an excellent visual carrier of surface structure. The surface is a prominent part

8.4. Difference in visual effect of same layout and different value. Right ABC demonstrates surface priority; left ABC, edge priority. *Photo courtesy of I. Magnin.*

of a viewer's attention. Imagine that same ABC all the same otherwise, but in black, the ABC on the left. The surface is not viewed the same and does not occupy the viewer's attention in the same way. The viewer does not even focus on surface but on edge. Thus the visual effect has changed even though only one definer, value, has been altered. Value is a controlling feature in this comparison.

MULTIPLE RELATIONSHIPS. The visual relations found in the ABC include both number of parts and their degree of connectedness. Many parts are related in more than one way. The form can be starkly simple or very intricate. Sometimes we notice single details, such as a red color or the length of trousers (especially when different from our past experiences). Details can combine and interrelate; for example, surfaces superimpose a shape on as well as interact with the leg.

The viewer must spend more time in viewing to attend to those parts or part properties that combine in more ways than one. Viewing the form involves seeing not just colors used but color and texture, not just surface but linear definition, not just the whole but the detail of the part.

Misunderstandings or simplistic interpretations are less likely to occur if we remain aware of the whole form and its potential relationships in a discovery process. Viewing takes time. As the viewer analyzes—compares uses of color, shape, and texture and relationships of parts to the whole—further discoveries will be made. Continual awareness will perpetuate more discovery, and curiosity will develop. A curious viewer will learn to fully understand a range of visual effects in the ABC.

SIMPLE AND COMPLEX FORMS. ABCs range from being visually simple to complex. When there are few relationships, viewers may become quickly bored. But even in ABCs that appear simple, the parts can relate in more than one way. Organization can result in varying degrees of dependence and independence of parts; the ABC that is successively ordered will appear simple.

Visual complexity should not be equated with the number of parts alone. When many parts can be counted, we may say the result is complex, but this confuses complexity with too much going on. Visual complexity also involves the connectedness and multiplicity of the visual relationships. At first this type of complexity may not be apparent; the viewer can even interpret the ABC as simple upon initial examination. After first attraction, however, attention is sustained by multiple, even subtle, visual

relations. This can occur when a definite order of parts simplifies the initial viewing and the form gives the effect of simplicity.

The function of the part

The viewer organizes the form by the process of comparing the similarities and differences in parts and the part with the whole. When part relationships compete in an ABC the clearest, most stable relations are the ones that will prevail. The viewer is initially attracted to those parts that offer the most contrast within the ABC. But the organizing process is also controlled by the similarity of parts and their relation to the whole.

An illustration of the way similarity and difference are used by the viewer in organizing is presented in figure 8.5.

The blouse in the ABC on the left contrasts with jacket value and this contrast becomes a source of focus at center front. But its similarity with the dark

8.5. ABCs with similarities and differences in visual parts, which direct the viewer. *Photos courtesy of University of Minnesota; photographer, Leo Perry.*

value of the skirt directs the viewer to examine their differences. The blouse on the right has a surface pattern that is similar to the other parts. Thus the viewer may not begin there but may first focus on the whole or on the shadow at center front. Eventually, the similarity in size of the surface shapes directs the viewer to examine and compare their similarities and differences. In this way the viewer is directed from one part to the other.

To understand the ABC is to become aware of our responses to all of its visual relations. We can understand how we organize a variety of parts by making conscious the process of grouping and separating and the function of the part within the ABC. Parts function differently— some function primarily as a source of priority and focus and some as a source of integration for the whole.

VIEWING PRIORITY. While we experience the wholeness of visual forms based upon similarities within them, what we first notice is a difference, a break from similarity. This difference can originate from the form itself or from the associations presented. (Refer to chap. 9 for discussion of relation of ideas.)

Parts viewed as separated are unlike their immediately adjacent surround, but the degree of separation varies. Parts can be different in any one or several of the visual definers or modifiers. A part may look clearly large because it is next to a small part. This contrast, which can be large with small, horizontal with vertical, light with dark, sharpens the perception of both. The sweater in figure 8.6 contrasts more within the whole than does the jacket or trousers and thereby attracts more attention.

As the viewer becomes aware of the part and its function in the whole, it can be manipulated. Its interaction with other parts can change the appearance of the whole. Imagine the lighter sweater in

8.6. A part attracts more attention when there is a higher degree of contrast of the part within the whole. The white diagonal shapes on the sweater become a source of focus because of relatively more contrast of the shapes within the whole. *Designed by Jhane Barnes; photographer, Albert Bray. Used by permission.*

figure 8.4 worn with black slacks and shoes on a dark-haired, dark-skinned person. By contrast, it becomes a priority part.

To contrast is to stand against. In comparing dissimilar parts, the viewer receives a clearer message of both parts if the dissimilarity is a distinct contrast. Rough next to smooth sharpens the meaning of both surfaces. Regular shapes next to irregular intensify the difference. All three of the dimensions of color—hue, value, and intensity—offer potential for visual contrast. A light value next to a dark will create a distinct visual separation. Cold hue against warm produces contrast in spatial position.

Contrast sets up counteraction in perception, a break in linkages. The viewer attempts to give the clearest meaning to what he sees. Parts that are clearly in contrast are given viewing priority. If the goal is to call attention to a smooth skin surface, place a rough surface next to it. If the goal is to call attention to a body part, put a part that is clearly different in shape and size next to it. By heightening the differences in visual parts, contrast can create a dramatic effect.

FOCUS. Visual parts can function within the whole as a source of focus. To serve as focus the part must be different in character from its context. The relation is one of contrast. In figure 8.3c value contrast makes the upper body area in the ABCs a priority.

Any part of the ABC can serve as a source of focus, but certain factors tend to be influential. For example, the strength of the part influences how it is viewed—as a primary or secondary source of focus. Parts may be grouped within a large area of the body and be separated from the remainder of the ABC. In figure 8.7 the upper torso pattern segregates from the grouping of the coat, trousers, and the continuous edge of silhouette. A part that is small and grouped but very isolated and different from its surround is a likely source of focus. An example are the buttons in figure 8.8.

CENTERING. Centering is viewing the ABC as having a convergent center focus. This can be a point or visual axis. A part that controls viewing is often essential to the visual order and meaning of the ABC. Priority can be achieved by placement on the body, by contrast in size or intensity of color.

Centering can occur because of lines radiating from a central point. The shapes of lapels can appear to converge as they angle into the first buttonhole

8.7. Value contrasts make the upper body area a visual priority in the ABC. *Photo courtesy of Andrew Fezza Menswear; photographer, Thom Gilbert.*

8.8. Buttons become focus and function to integrate two areas of contrast within the ABC. *Photo courtesy of Bill Blass, Ltd.; photographer, Gideon Lewin.*

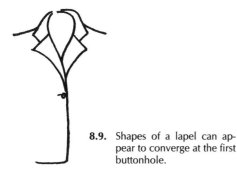

8.9. Shapes of a lapel can appear to converge at the first buttonhole.

(fig. 8.9). Triangular or wedge-shaped folds placed on the body often create a center by converging at an apex. If they do not quite converge, the lines may still be viewed as doing so, incorporating the immediately adjacent area (fig. 8.10).

8.10. Triangular shapes create a focus at the center of the upper torso. *Photo courtesy of University of Nebraska; Jinger Eberspacher, designer and model.*

Centering can describe the visual axis created by the interaction of parts within the ABC. Placement of a group of parts, a line of buttons or a fold of the fabric, close to the vertical axis of the body attracts the viewer's eye to the center of the body (see snowflake sweater, fig. 7.16b). A sweater contrasting with its jacket but similar to the color of the pants can create a centering on the body. A viewer can group the lines created by a tie, vest, and sweater (fig. 8.11a, b).

a   b

8.11. **a.** Viewer groups the dark value of the sweater and the pants to create a center. **b.** Viewer groups similar lines created by a tie and the band on a sweater to create a center. *Photos courtesy of Jones New York.*

We tend to view the horizontal axis of the body as the widest area from one body view. The horizontal axis of the body without clothes may be the shoulders, especially when a head with closely shaped hair creates contrast with the width of the shoulders, or it may be the hip area when the hands or wrists continue the hipline at crotch level. Clothing can emphasize such a horizontal axis or change it. Shoulder pads will emphasize the horizontal axis at the shoulder. A cape that flares away from the body at the hem, ending at the wrist, can emphasize the horizontal axis at the hipline.

123

The vertical and horizontal axes may cross and create a strong center point or area, or one may be dominant. The silhouette shape helps to determine this centering but the parts within are also determining factors.

CONTROLLING RELATIONSHIPS. The viewer's task in understanding organization is to determine what is causing a part to group and/or separate and further what controls the relationship between parts. This involves observing their degree of similarity.

In any one ABC there can be a number of visual parts with varying degrees of separation. A visual part that is viewed as very independent, very much separated from the context of the ABC, is likely to be functioning as a point of contrast and focus. A substantial degree of separation of the part is critical in establishing its priority.

A part may be separate enough to create focus but still similar enough to another part to direct the viewer in the organizing process. The visual part that is similar in only one definer, such as value, can still direct the viewer to that similarity in the next part. In figure 8.3a the tie at the neck in the ABC on the right can group with the hair, the belt, and the shoes because of similar value. The striped polo shirt in the ABC on the left can group with similar dark hair, skin, and belt. Thus the part is first identified and then considered for those definers and/or modifiers that control the organizing process.

A visual part that is viewed as interdependent with its surround is often being grouped in perception with other parts and functioning in an integrating sense. Parts are often related in several or even many different ways within the whole. An observer may connect a part first with a part similar in one property and then with a part similar in another.

The degree of similarity will influence the organizing process.

A part, as you remember, may be grouped with another part because of any of the Gestalt organizing factors—similarity, closure, proximity, continuation—or the modifiers—number, size, visual weight, and spatial position. Two parts may group because their boundaries appear continuous. When hair is shaped to create a line that continues the line of a collar or lapel, the viewer groups by perceiving their similarity either through closure or continuation (fig. 8.12).

Parts that vary in degree of similarity also vary in their coherence to one another. If parts are similar in several definers, for example, the viewer groups the parts more easily. A part may be similar in shape as well as in hue and surface

8.12. Viewer groups by perceiving similarity of surface and closure. *Photo courtesy of Polyester Fashion Council.*

texture. Such parts would group easily for the viewer because the visual relation would be clear, the connection primary.

When part relationships compete in an ABC the simplest and clearest organization will prevail, that is, the relation will prevail that is easiest to view. This means a part clear in its spatial position, that is, one that clearly lies on top of another, will be noticed before one that is not. Parts ambiguous in their relation to one another take longer to organize.

To become aware of all the ways a part will group takes time. The viewer must continue to refer to the entirety of the ABC. Since most have habitual and favorite ways of viewing, e.g., a shoe seller starting with the feet, we must continually remind ourselves of the whole.

INTEGRATION. A visual part that functions as a source of integration does so because of its similarity to other parts within the context of the ABC. The part may not attract attention to itself but functions to group with another part or direct attention within the ABC.

Integration results from parts that are viewed as interdependent. Similarity promotes integration. For example, in figure 8.2a the band acts to integrate the whole because of similar value with the skirt and similar shape with the neckline and buttons. If a number of similar shapes are viewed throughout the body, the ABC will appear integrated because the viewer will be directed to the whole (fig. 8.1c). Some of those shapes may be different in color; this directs the viewer to group similar colors. A shiny texture of black patent leather shoes may be repeated in a satin stripe defining the trouser seam of a tuxedo. Reflection from each surface integrates the whole because the viewer compares the similarity of shine.

Part blending. Integration results from parts that blend, that is, one part is not more dominant than another. Soft edges help to blend visual parts. Soft edges can result from similarity in any one of the definers. For example, two parts similar in value or texture may not attract attention to themselves as much as to the whole form, especially if the whole form is closed from the surround. Yet the intricacy of viewing such a subtle relation is important to the visual result (fig. 8.1b).

Part gradation. Gradation has been defined as a measured difference in a part-to-part relation. Gradation can be a source of integration by directing the eye either within one body view or around the body. Examples can occur using many visual definers and modifiers—light to medium to dark value, hard to soft edge, small to large shape, rough to smooth texture. The visual measure varies in closely graded intervals from one part to the next; the parts vary by degree. When this happens the eye is directed by the difference between the parts or part properties from one adjacent part to another (fig. 8.2b).

Transition part. A transition part functions as an interval between two otherwise contrasting parts. It can make the transition by softening their contrast with a repetition of one of each of their attributes. For example, two parts totally contrasting in value placed side by side are viewed as separating. A necklace of small areas of both black and white can serve as a transition between the two parts (fig. 8.13). In figure 8.8 buttons

8.13. A necklace consisting of small areas of black and white can serve as a transition between two contrasting parts. *Photo courtesy of Bill Blass, Ltd.; photographer, Gideon Lewin.*

function to integrate two areas of contrast.

Viewing the ABC

If the process of organizing parts is followed routinely, awareness of visual relationships should become second nature in viewing a form. Knowing about these relationships can lead to discoveries about the visual effect of an ABC.

VIEWING PATH. The direction taken while scanning the ABC is the viewing path. If the viewer numbers the parts in order of viewing, the path can be noted. The visual path may encircle the ABC or remain within one body view, rounded or flat viewing. The cues of the ABC greatly influence the direction of the path (fig. 8.14).

8.14. Viewing begins at the center of the body and then moves vertically to the skirt and horizontally to the jacket. *Designed by Pauline Trigere. Used by permission.*

The visual path can take a number of different directions within one body view (fig. 8.15). The path may be related to the vertical or horizontal axis of the body, with the dominant direction being either vertical or horizontal. The visual path can be curvilinear on the vertical or horizontal plane and still be directed within the one body view.

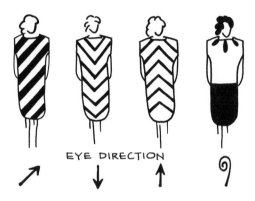

8.15. The visual path can take a number of different directions within one body view.

The body axis plays an important role in the scanning process. The vertical axis of the body can serve as the center in viewing the ABC. Even when a vertical line is placed slightly off center, the resulting tension is a reference to the vertical axis. The vertical reference can be an implied line. It can be shapes forming a continuous line on the vertical axis through size variation, or it can be color or texture gradation. Color gradation, beginning with a light value on top, progressing to medium to dark value on the bottom, can be the source of the viewing path. Thus, the viewer needs to consider broadly which one or several of the definers or modifiers could be the reason for the vertical direction.

Horizontal lines and shapes contrast the basic verticality of the body and are often strong viewing references. But the viewer needs to consider the direction of the viewing path and not the direction of the lines. For example, if a series of horizontal lines extend to the silhouette and vary from wide to narrow, their gradation may be what directs the viewer. Then the viewing path would be vertical. When horizontal lines are viewed as extending around the body cylinder (often accompanied by rounded surfaces), the viewing path would be horizontal.

8.17.
Viewing priority can occur with silhouette edge or surface.

THE ENTRY. Where we first enter the ABC—our first focus—is important to note. This is often the area of most contrast either in terms of part properties or our expectations.

Our visual scan may be concentrated within one part that has viewing priority (fig. 8.16). Certain parts or part properties may take priority in viewing an ABC and this priority can influence the way the ABC is perceived. When part-to-whole viewing occurs, is the cause clear edge definition of simple shapes or a contrast of surface that overrides the effect of the silhouette as a whole or some other combination of factors (fig. 8.17)?

The ABC may be viewed as a whole first because of the interdependence of the parts or because of the distinctness of the silhouette. The degree of correspondence between the frame of the ABC and its details or parts can make a difference in whether a part stands out in perception or whether it becomes integrated. A

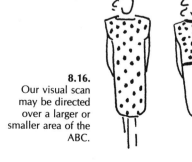

8.16.
Our visual scan may be directed over a larger or smaller area of the ABC.

closed silhouette can become a viewing priority. A repeated shape with some degree of planar separation that covers a large area can refer the viewer to the whole. The viewer does not attend to each shape as a separate part.

CAUSE OF VISUAL EFFECT. What causes the viewer to organize the ABC? It may be a priority part or part property such as a dominant surface or edge. In viewing the whole ABC we may first concentrate on the shape of a large part but then secondly focus on some unexpected surface treatment.

As one part is compared with another, the viewer can read the ABC primarily as a two-dimensional surface, with the variation of the parts occurring on one level or on several levels in the space between the ABC and the viewer, planar integration or segregation. The viewer can take in the entire ABC or remain in one area—whole-to-part viewing or part-to-whole. The viewer can also read the ABC as a three-dimensional surface without separating into figure and ground.

An in-depth analysis of similarities and differences in visual parts within the whole helps the viewer to understand the cause of the visual effect. The analysis should continue comparing uses of color, shape, and texture and their interaction. A viewer can be directed by a

8.18.
A point of focus may direct the viewer when accompanied by a similar point along the vertical axis of the body.

definer or a modifier. It can be the difference in a part, perceived at entry, that causes the viewer to compare the part with another (fig. 8.18). A viewer can be directed by a visual part or parts, including body parts.

That which directs the viewer is often not obvious at first. For example, the influence of light and shadow variations could be missed. A surface that is structured with a strong planar contrast may be used in the ABC. If the shapes are redundant, the viewing path may be influenced more by the silhouette than by the shapes as figure. Sometimes the visual part is similar to other parts in all respects except one (e.g., location within silhouette), and it takes some thought to analyze exactly what is directing the viewer (fig. 8.19).

THE TEMPORAL SEQUENCE. The point in time when a part comes into the viewer's awareness depends on the viewing order, or temporal sequence. By numbering the areas of focus as they are viewed, the viewer has a good indication of temporal sequence. In viewing the ABC it helps to be aware of temporal sequence because it is a quick means of determining viewing priorities.

An ABC can present different priorities for the viewer. One part can connect in a number of ways with other parts, and the viewer takes in these connecting links in the order in which they attract

his or her attention. The viewer may perceive several or many groupings. For example, an ABC may be viewed first in terms of a light yellow shirt and handkerchief contrasting with a navy blue jacket. Next the ABC is viewed in terms of two rows of brass buttons grouping at center front and finally in terms of similarity in the dark value of hair and jacket. Being conscious of viewing sequence will greatly help the viewer in understanding the ABC as well as in becoming aware of its priorities and controlling features. The ABC at first may appear quite simple. Upon further examination the subtleties—those parts that integrate with several other parts—become evident.

The viewer needs to be aware of the entirety of the ABC to perceive subtleties. An ABC involving a dark gray suit can demontrate this principle. A head of light-value hair and light-value skin may be grouped first with a light blouse that contrasts with the suit. The rest of the body may be skimmed according to the contrasting silhouette. In carefully

8.19. An ABC viewed in terms of similarities and contrasts in shapes and values. *Photo courtesy of University of Minnesota; designed by Vicki Johnson.*

viewing the whole ABC, the viewer may notice the shape of the pockets is similar to the shape of the sleeves and lapels. Thus, the viewing order in an ABC is not only what first attracts a viewer's attention but also what sustains it.

By considering order through temporal sequence, the viewer recognizes that some parts of the ABC take priority in viewing and it is important to understand this priority. But at the same time, it is still important to perceive the entire ABC. The viewer who stops with the priority parts may not understand the visual effect of the ABC.

THE VIEWING TEMPO. The rate at which the viewer takes in the ABC is the viewing tempo. This term refers to the amount and type of activity taking place within an ABC and the resulting effect on the viewer. The pace can be immediate and abrupt or lingering.

An ABC that is simple and bold, viewed as a whole first, with a hard-edged determinate surface is likely to have an immediacy in viewing and its visual path clearly marked. The viewer takes such an ABC in quickly. An ABC that has many contrasting and independent parts is viewed at a little slower pace than the first example. Even though this ABC is ordered, there is more complexity because of the viewing of separate parts first. The viewer gets caught up in a process of spotting the breaks from repetition, the contrasts within the whole. An ABC with many blending parts can be viewed as a whole but at a smooth and lingering pace.

KINDS OF ORGANIZATION. There are patterns of order from which we can generalize. The ABC may appear to have a definite viewing sequence or appear less ordered, even random, as the viewer takes in separate parts (fig. 8.20). Both of these types of ordering can occur in

8.20.
An ABC may be viewed as a sequence of parts or more equal random parts.

levels. We can also organize the parts by grouping of like units in levels appearing on top of or superimposed upon ground. Another ABC may appear to be viewed as a whole first but later in terms of surface intricacy. We can organize the ABC in its primary relatedness of surface to an adjacent surface—by a side-to-side comparison within a single plane. These patterns of order are considered in the following discussion.

ORDER IN LEVELS OR SIDE BY SIDE. We can organize several parts or groups of parts on different planes between the ABC and the viewer, i.e., planar segregation. Initially the parts group by similarity, but then the layers of parts are ordered by their separation from the whole. The visual effect is that of a breakup of the space of the ABC (fig. 8.21).

A surface printed with colored shapes of yellow, red, and dark blue on a black ground would tend to be grouped in layers of figure. We might group in order of most contrasting to least contrasting in value, first the yellow shapes, then the red, then the dark blue. Figure 8.22 is an ABC viewed in terms of large to small size of figure and proximity of similar shapes. The surfaces appear to be on different planar levels.

Parts that are more equivalent are organized in a side-by-side manner (fig. 8.12). The order is based on the similar-

8.21.
Parts of ABCs can be viewed as side by side or layered.

Both planar levels and side-by-side part relations can occur within one ABC (fig. 8.23). The viewer needs to be aware of both possibilities. Vital to what we perceive is the relation of part to part in terms of such factors as number, location, strength, and position in space, both single plane and illusion of separate planes.

SIMULTANEOUS, SUCCESSIVE, OR SEPARATED. In our viewing we may find the whole or the parts simpler to perceive. We will tend to perceive that which has the most clarity first of all.

When the whole is simpler to perceive, that is called simultaneous viewing. This does not necessarily mean that is all there is to see. Often the surfaces are primary in their relations of light and shadow or indeterminacy that create a side-by-side comparison of the intricacy (fig. 8.1).

In the process of perceiving the

ity of parts that leads from one to another. This relatedness can occur because of a gradual change throughout the ABC (fig.8.1a). The comparison from one part to another directs the viewing path. Parts are not different enough to cause independence and separation. For example, a wide line may get narrower very gradually. The size of a part may vary slightly from larger to smaller throughout the ABC. A surface texture may vary gradually.

As the viewer observes the ABC, attention may be directed to the surfaces as they refer to the body in-the-round. The viewer perceives the ABC as a three-dimensional form. The entire ABC may be viewed according to surfaces that lead the eye around the ABC. The difference to the visual effect is that the body appears as a whole form. Attention is sustained by surface variation and the interdependence of the parts with the whole.

8.22. An ABC that is viewed in layers based upon large to small size of figure and proximity of similar shapes. *Photo courtesy of Adrienne Vittadini; winter/fall jacquard—stripes and pattern inspired by ethnic basketry.*

8.23. Parts may be ordered as they appear side by side and on planar levels. *Photo courtesy of University of Minnesota; designed by Linda Joette Sawochka; model, Mary Elleson-Jones.*

whole ABC, the viewer may find that some parts have a clear priority. When a part has priority, some kind of sequence is established in our viewing. Parts that have unequal visual weight create a sequential ordering. Parts that have an equal visual weight but are located at a distance from one another can create successive viewing.

When two viewers comparing their visual path in an ABC identify the same parts first, second, and third, the parts are usually successively ordered. When parts exist in a hierarchy and are viewed in a sequence, the whole can appear simple because each part has its place (fig. 8.2).

An ABC can be less definite in its order, too. For example, two viewers may agree on what is the visual path but not on the precise viewing order. For exam-

ple, both viewers may enter the viewing process from a different point but proceed in a similar path. This ABC is still ordered but less sequentially. Some parts are equal and some are unequal and independent.

An ABC organized first as parts that are more separated usually has several equivalent parts (fig. 8.3). The parts are more independent and give the viewer a part-to-whole impression. When the viewer considers visual path, this ABC is often viewed more casually.

A separated effect may occur for a variety of reasons. For example, the silhouette of the ABC may be a continuous straight line, and the parts are viewed in a curving path. The shapes of the silhouette and the parts may be about equal visually, and the choice of either of the two gives the effect of a randomness to the viewing process. Irregular and organic shapes on the surface that separate as figure can also be viewed individually (fig. 8.23).

Sometimes the parts of the ABC appear ordered, but the cause is not immediately apparent because the viewer is not aware of or does not understand the visual connections between parts. Continued efforts to include the causes of order can broaden one's viewing experience.

Thus the organizational process involves strategies in viewing the ABC. The process can be described in objective terms based upon the interaction of the viewer with the form. The visual relationships within the ABC can be understood in terms of their effect on this organization.

Visual exercises

I. Analyzing the visual order of the ABC.
  A. Select two ABCs that appear to be very different in as many visual aspects as possible.
  B. Discuss functions of part-to-part-to-whole ABCs in terms of ordering. Discuss why the two ABCs appear to be different.
  C. Find examples of two ABCs that differ in their visual order, one in which the parts are unequal creating a definite visual path that another observer and you would both follow. Determine the visual path and then compare your choice with that of another observer.
  D. Now find an ABC in which the parts are more equal, creating a less clearcut visual path. Again determine the visual path and compare with another observer.
  E. Discuss and justify your selections in C and D.

9

Interpreting the ABC: associations of meaning

IN a systematic approach to understanding the ABC, the observer must understand how meaning is given to what is perceived. Meaning is derived from the many associations the viewer must make to relate a particular ABC to self and surround. These associations can range from those that are unique to the viewer to those that are universally shared. An educated viewer is one who can interpret a specific ABC by recognizing these associations and their relation to the ABC.

The form, the situation, and the observer all contribute to the interpretation of the ABC. The form is the source of many associations: the particular color, texture, and shape, the method of organization—all can result in distinctive visual effects. The visual form can stimulate and guide the observer's perception; in turn the observer can interpret the form through associations that come from past and present experiences. In this chapter we will concentrate on how the form is interpreted according to the associations that influence the visual effect.

Sources of associations

Meaning associations are primary in perceiving a visual form and are quite automatic. Meaning results from a form that has specific visual relations resulting in a distinct visual effect. Such associations can develop at a subconscious level, in which case we do not become conscious of them or examine their relation to the form. This becomes a problem in interpretation because the viewer needs to find some way for associations to be consciously considered.

The potential for associations that can be made while perceiving the ABC are abundant. A *look,* or expected viewing pattern, can be established based on an association the viewer has of the form as it relates to a time or an event. To be knowledgeable about such viewing patterns means the viewer is not only aware of their existence but is always in the process of discovering the combinations that occur repeatedly. Some forms are the source of more distinctive meanings than others. Some designers of ABCs capture a share of the clothing market because of their consistency in creating forms that elicit similar and distinct meanings. It is very revealing to study forms of a particular designer or market according to their consistent meanings.

SUBTLE OR BOLD. Past experiences of the viewer in perceiving the ABC establish certain viewing patterns. A viewer who recognizes established viewing patterns becomes more knowledgeable and able to recognize more subtle associations. The more the viewer searches for such viewing patterns, the easier it becomes to recognize them. By exercising the ability to make associations, the educated viewer finds that what was subtle becomes bold and explicit.

The viewer who notes a subtlety of form is often the one who knows enough to pick out the specific details that offer interpretation. For example, the curved stitching on a pocket may represent a brand of jeans widely known to a social group, but the meaning of an elaboration of the stitching is understood only by a smaller group. The message may be understated because either few know about it or it involves only one small aspect of the ABC. However, as more and more viewers learn to pay attention to the association, it will become visually more important. An example would be a minute label on the sleeve of a t-shirt or, during a time of war, the increased rec-

ognition of heroes by reference to a small shirt decoration.

Differences can be recognized between associations that are pretty commonly understood by other viewers with similar experiences and those that are "unique to me." An ABC may mean something to two people because of its associations with their lives but also be universal in its appeal to those same associations in other people's experiences. For example, a ring on the third finger of the left hand is associated with attachment; it has both a personal and a universal meaning. The degree to which the form suggests meaning can vary from mere hints to exaggeration (fig. 9.1).

Over time the ABC changes, associations change, and related meanings change. What was once obvious and bold becomes insignificant. We keep current in our interpretations only by

9.1.
Meaning can be directly evidenced in the ABC. **a.** Reference to football. *Photo courtesy of Fairchild Visuals, division of Fairchild Publications, Inc., New York City.* **b.** Reference to the Orient. *Photo courtesy of Minneapolis College of Art and Design; designed by Nancy Orenstein.* **c.** Reference to western United States, primarily from hats, boots, and ties. *Photo courtesy of Fairchild Visuals, division of Fairchild Publications, Inc., New York City.*

a

b

c

maintaining an awareness of their link with specific surfaces, edges, and spaces. For example, historically black used for clothing has been a sign of mourning, but today we interpret its use as a strong dramatic statement associated with maturity. Thus the educated viewer needs to be aware of the current associations of the features of an ABC.

SINGLE OR RELATIONAL. Associations can be related to single properties found in the form. Warm colors, such as red or yellow, may relate directly to a feeling of gaiety, for example. A vertical line repeats the upright position of the body and the dignity of the human condition. A curved shape is said to suggest a softening of the body and is often associated with the female gender, while angularity is often considered male.

Associations can also be related to the way the form properties are combined into specific surfaces and edges to create a particular visual effect. In fact many such associations are so common, they have been named and taken for granted. The term *blazer* refers to a covering for the upper torso with specific and characteristic lines and shapes. The way in which the ABC is organized is a further source of distinct visual effect. We give labels to distinct patterns of organization that result in common meanings, such as youthful, sophisticated, sexy.

One association we take for granted is recognition of the form character as it relates to the wearer, i.e., identification of an ABC as belonging to a specific age, gender, occupation, ethnic group. This is a task that we must carry out just to get along in a societal group and that is often taken for granted. In fact we may not even notice what specific surfaces, edges, and motions are associated with each category. For example, for woman we could specify young, rich, or friendly.

9.2. Traditional male and female visual forms. *Bridesmaid gown from Dance-Allure; tuxedo by After Six. Used by permission.*

How does an ABC look friendly or rich through color, texture, shape? What combinations trigger a particular visual result?

To interpret an ABC the viewer may need to become involved in a viewing pattern with many complex associations. For example, *androgyny* is a term applied to the ABC that includes both male and female associations. But understanding androgyny requires first understanding what it means to appear female and male. What viewing patterns result in the visual effect of femaleness or maleness? Traditional female form characteristics can include openness of silhouette, planar integration, light surface values, and simultaneous viewing. Male form characteristics can include closed forms, planar separation, determinate surfaces, and successive viewing (fig. 9.2). Androgyny in the ABC would derive from a mixing of male and female form characteristics, for example, an open silhouette with determinate surfaces in a light value.

PERCEPTIBLE OR INFERRED. Meaning can be derived from properties directly perceptible in the form. Associations can be explicit because they correspond directly to readily perceived features such as line, shape, color, or surface texture. Such directly perceptible properties can help determine meaning of an ABC.

Associations also include those that are indirect and inferred, where meaning is only suggested from the form structure. Such an indirect association is called a *symbol*. One idea or thing can stand for another. Names, for example, can represent objects or persons. They can stand for categories, variations, and properties of objects. Carriers of symbolic meaning can be flags, money, words that are in common use among people who interact with each other. They are determined within a culture and therefore may vary among cultures.

Previous experiences with clothing can influence associations. We categorize basic articles of apparel, such as shirt, blazer, trousers, because of our experience of separateness of these items in dressing, in purchasing. We all have experienced the different body motions of putting on a shirt or trousers or a skirt. We often purchase apparel as separate items, labeling them accordingly. Thus even though the apparel items are not perceived individually, rather as a portion of a whole, the separateness is inferred.

Since symbolic meanings are a less direct reference to the ABC, the viewer must look beyond the form for interpretation. This does not mean the form structure should be ignored, however. Symbolic associations are initiated by something viewed in the ABC.

Associations can imitate either the properties found in other natural or manmade objects or property relationships. In present viewing we continually look for similarities to previously experienced objects. A common example is the continual search for meaning in cloud formations. We see a similarity to horses,

bells, people. In the ABC a shape can resemble a leaf or a leopard spot. The viewer can refer to a color as being blue as the sky, red as a rose, or similar to the earth. When an association derives from an imitation of something observed before, a football player or a penguin, we often compare the similarities.

The form structure can become symbolic of cultural values. For example, a look has been identified from the following combination: a two-piece suit with a determinate medium-to-dark value surface, a light-colored shirt, and dark tie or bow. This look is not only distinctive as a form, but to adopt this look, that is, to wear apparel of this type, has come to signify an acceptance of traditional American values.

The ABC may combine both perceptible and inferred associations. For example, in the United States a young boy is identified as a Cub Scout when he is wearing a dark blue shirt with many badges of gold and other multicolored patches. The association identifying the young boy as a Scout is directly perceptible in the form, based upon similar past experiences of the viewer. But such a form has also become associated with trustworthiness, perhaps because the organization is commonly known to promote trust.

Thus, understanding the sources of associations is necessary to the interpretation of the ABC. Associations that are automatic and unconscious need to be brought to awareness. The viewer who becomes skilled in recognizing them can begin to understand the form and its potential for meaning. To identify these sources does take practice, but the ability can be developed. Now let us look at how knowledge of the sources of association can be applied to specific considerations of the form, the viewer, and the situation.

Form associations— expressive effect

Interpretation involves understanding those traits that summarize the form itself, that distinguish it from other forms. This is the unifying idea of the ABC—the fusion of the separate parts into a whole. This unifying idea is referred to as its message, its meaning, expressive effect, or character.

What characteristics of the ABC can be interpreted as unifying ideas? Sources of fusion can arise directly from the form itself. The way we view the ABC involves not only how we look with our eyes and minds but how we feel about what we see. What feelings can be elicited from the way the form is organized by the viewer? Expressive effects arise from those properties of the ABC that are perceptible to the viewer, what we have identified as the definers and modifiers in previous chapters. The way these form properties associate in the whole influences expressive effect.

Expressive effects are those fusions that lead us to such feelings as excitement or calmness, strength or delicacy. These emotions can derive from the ABC and are inferred from the relations of the form properties. Basic elementary mental states can be linked directly to the feelings arising from perceiving the ABC. Below is a listing of some form properties that can work together and often bring about expressions of excitement, calmness, strength, or delicacy.

Excitement

Shape: simple, contrasting, several to many

Line: discontinuous, diagonal, zigzag

Color: intense warm primary hues, contrasts in value

Texture: smooth surfaces that do not interrupt edge viewing or filled surfaces that do.

Viewing priority may be open form, part to whole, planar separation, rounded, and determinate and indeterminate.

Calmness

Shape: few with little contrast between or clear hierarchy

Line: continuous and mostly related to the body axis

Color: muted, neutrals, cool colors

Texture: smooth surfaces with uninterrupted edge viewing, subtle background

Viewing priority may be closed form, whole to part, planar integration, rounded, and determinate.

Strength

Shape: large, with silhouette emphasis

Line: continuous, directed, dominant, thick, bold

Color: value contrast, dark colors, neutral light

Texture: smooth surfaces to edge, very coarse textured areas often used in combination with smooth, dark surfaces or in unusual combinations

Viewing priority may be closed form, whole to part, planar separation, flat, and determinate.

Delicacy

Shape: small, rounding, soft edge

Line: curved, discontinuous, light weight

Color: clear warm colors, tints of warm or cool colors

Texture: minute variations, often printed and blurred

Viewing priority may be open form, part to whole, planar integration, rounded, and indeterminate.

The interaction of the form properties can result in an expression that is a powerful influence on visual effect (fig. 9.3). That is, the meaning derives from form

a

b

c

d

9.3. Expressive effects from the ABC can include **a.** Excitement. *Photo courtesy of Fairchild Visuals, division of Fairchild Publications, Inc., New York City.* **b.** Calmness. *Evening dress from the Fall 1985 Collection of Morton Myles for the Warrens; designed by Morton Myles. Used by permission.* **c.** Strength. *Designed by Morton Myles. Used by permission.* **d.** Delicacy. *Photo courtesy of University of Minnesota, Goldstein Gallery; photographer, Judy Olausen.*

properties and the associations they create within the whole. The form can be described as relating to separable components. For example, an ABC can be described as red or vertical or softened by the curves of a shape (fig. 9.4a, b *color section*).

Expressive effects are also influenced by the ordering of the ABC. For example, the observer would tend to perceive part to whole for the exciting and delicate effects and whole to part for the calm and strong effects. The viewing priority of the ABC would influence the expressive effect; for example, the effect of excitement might be created by open, part-to-whole, rounded, and indeterminate surfaces and by figure-ground contrast or even reversals (fig. 9.5).

When an ABC is described as dramatic or businesslike, expressive effect is being labeled. Such an effect is the result of a fusion of form properties. Dramatic may describe a fusion of the whole com-

bining properties of both the exciting and strong categories; businesslike may describe a fusion of the whole combining properties of the calm and strong categories.

Characterizing the ABC involves a recognition of unifying ideas or themes, even though the specific form properties that make them recognizable may vary. For example, an ABC recognized as a business look will usually have a range of acceptable associated properties. The viewer would be able to recognize a business look even though the color changed. This may require generalizations about color. For example, a business look is often a neutral, middle-to-dark value matte surface. It often includes a background color repeating one of the body colors of the wearer. Thus the color may vary within a range of colors. Identification of expressive effect is not one color or one line but the way they are related—the way they fuse into an idea.

We derive meaning as a result of the expressive effects of the ABC. The form can be better understood by an explicit consideration of just what form properties are involved in the formation of a specific expressive effect. Thus, as we consider meaning, we need to keep these basic expressive effects and their associated form properties in mind.

Viewer associations

ATTENTION: PREDICTABILITY AND SURPRISE.

If an ABC is to attract and hold attention it requires both (1) expected or predictable visual relations accepted by the viewer and (2) surprise, or the reliance on some unexpected part or combination of parts to achieve interest, newness, or freshness. An observer's expectations regarding the ABC derive from his past experiences with visual forms, and

9.5. A sweater can express excitement. *Photo courtesy of Neiman-Marcus; photographer, Gordon Munro.*

the formation of these expectations is influenced by how much and what type of attention the viewer has given to visual forms.

Predictability arises out of the pleasure a viewer gains from recognition. A satisfying experience is something we like to see repeated. However, with repetition can come boredom if the object of our attention includes nothing stimulating or unexpected. After several repetitions of identical stimuli, the object becomes ground noise, that is, it no longer stimulates at the same level in attracting our attention. Soon it becomes background and not focus in our attention.

How do these two, predictability and surprise, work together? An example of how they interrelate can be given using a standard shirt. We expect it to have certain layout features: a collar, a yoke, a center front button closing, pockets in a horizontal line across the upper chest, short sleeves or long with a buttoned cuff. Surfaces predictably would be a light value and possess a small background pattern in a cotton broadcloth. We expect such a shirt to be worn under a sweater or jacket. Now what could be considered a surprise? A subtle change could be made by lowering the yoke line in the front and back. Such a change would affect the predictability, but the shirt form would not change so much that we would no longer recognize "shirtness." What could be a more major surprise? The shirt could possess an unexpected surface and be worn differently on the body, e.g., two sizes too large. The observer would still have to recognize the "shirtness" for this to remain in the predictability-surprise domain.

The typical observer attends first to the surprising aspects of an ABC. Since many ABCs have predictable aspects, the viewer has collected image patterns of expected relations. These are used as a base to speed up the perceptual process.

Whether the viewer chooses to concentrate on these expected patterns or on the surprising components is somewhat dependent upon his or her point of view. But the surprising aspects will be noticed by the viewer who has chosen to become knowledgeable about that form.

Predictability is based upon learning and knowing expected patterns of the ABC. How does a viewer learn to recognize expected patterns? The viewer must become interested in following the visual transformation of the ABC in some respect. For example, an editor of fashion is skilled in comparing past forms with new ones. Descriptions are couched in terms of comparison such as "a softer, more fitted look." What does that mean? you ask. Softer than what? The fashion editor is assuming an audience who has followed identifying features of fashion over time and who understands the comparison. Perhaps visual examples are included, photos or sketches; then the reader can also surmise from examining them what is meant by softer and more fitted.

If the observer is interested in a particular form and has followed its transformations, an expectancy develops from this experience. A jogger knows about running shoes because he has educated himself about running shoes. He reads an article on the new ideas in running equipment. He listens to sales personnel tell about the features of the particular shoes he really should try because they will surely be superior to the ones he has. The reference again is to the observer's past experience.

DEGREE OF SURPRISE. The surprising aspects of the form may be blatant or subtle. There is pleasure in being able to pick out the subtlety of a form, in following the nuance of change that occurs in a product. A viewer who doesn't know the product would not necesssarily recognize a subtlety unless it was pointed out. A change, such as a trend in mixing patterns within the ABC, could occur from one season to another. A change could also occur because of a technical development, such as an improvement in the shape of ski boots.

The relation of expectancy to surprise is one of degree—at one extreme is total surprise and at the other total predictability. The ABC may include mostly predictable associations, with a new color combination being the only varying or surprising feature. Focus then is on the color since the other aspects of structure follow expectations of the audience.

If the element of surprise is greater than this, the observer may be required to change viewing patterns in looking at the ABC. Instead of focusing on the silhouette as a priority, for example, the observer may have to focus on surface details to get the intended message. The observer may not be ready for the change and may not have adjusted viewing patterns. Understanding the form may require a major change in observational patterns. This factor could influence the success or failure of an ABC. How much change will the viewing audience tolerate?

MESSAGE CONGRUITY. Messages arise out of the predictability and surprise the viewer experiences. These messages can arise from one definer of the ABC or from the whole form. For example, expectations for combining visual texture might be the combination of determinate with determinate surfaces or of indeterminate with determinate. Then when the viewer perceives indeterminate with indeterminate, the message is not congruous with expectations and the response may be one of surprise.

When expectations are met we experience message congruity. For example, a tuxedo is congruous when it meets our expectations of a man's two-piece black jacket with satin collar, white shirt, black bow tie, and black trousers with stripes down the sides. We would also expect black shoes and socks. However, the message is incongruous when laced with a surprise—the tuxedo is all there but the feet have neon-colored socks. Our expectations are met, except for the feet, which jar us out of our unconscious expectations.

Often the ABC relies on mixed messages for timeliness. For example, an ABC could involve a white satin shirt with blue jeans or a frilly lace collar on an otherwise traditional khaki military uniform. We are thus jarred from the viewing reverie that arises out of the expectation of message congruity (fig. 9.6).

The observer will interpret the ABC on the basis of expectancies. In turn, the message of the unexpected is a way to

9.6. An ABC whose message is based upon surprise. *Photo courtesy of Fairchild Visuals, division of Fairchild Publications, Inc., New York City.*

9.7. An ABC that expresses whimsical sophistication. *Photo courtesy of University of Minnesota; designed by Georgia Scheu.*

gain the attention of a particular observer. For example, in figure 9.7 the ABC gains attention because it is a mixture of the whimsical with sophistication. The clown shapes on the tabard appear joyous and are in contrast with the dark-value stripes on the remainder of the ABC. However, a viewer could enjoy this ABC regardless of whether the connotations were recognized. Interpretation will depend upon the observer's own expectancies, interests, education, as well as upon the situation and surrounding conditions of observation.

INDIVIDUAL AND SHARED MEANING. Is perception of meaning a totally individual and personal experience? If so, how is meaning shared? How does communication take place? The answer lies in a recognition of the differences between meaning of the ABC related to unique personal experiences and to culturally shared experiences. Individual experiences may be unique but similar to the individual experiences of others, therefore expressions of the universal. Often a basic similarity can be observed in several viewers' responses toward the same ABC. When observers can agree upon an interpretation of its basic form, social usage establishes common associations.

The educated viewer needs to be aware of the difference between a personal but universal experience and a merely personal one. We can distinguish from our own experiences those that could have similar meanings for other observers. Visual forms throughout history have been based upon the premise of the universal, that visual forms can communicate shared meaning to a culture as well as to an individual.

The observer can distinguish which associations are socially established, which are individual but universal, and which are totally unique. All of these distinctions come from the observer's own past experience. To perceive and interpret associations from a broader sociocultural point of view means to emphasize the aspects that could have similar meanings for other observers. To say not only, This is what it means to me, but also, This is what it means, implies a generalization of social meaning: This is what it means to a contemporary, educated, and knowing society.

Situational associations

Commonality of experience occurs within a group, be it a small group or a large group within a society. Our similar experiences become shared sources of association to the ABC. Some of the sources of shared experiences are very influential in formation of our response to the ABC. They are the situational associations related to a viewer's surroundings or milieu. These are discussed as the influence of culture, time, and event.

CULTURAL MILIEU. Unifying ideas of the ABC are related to that which is important and therefore seeks expression within a culture. If youthfulness is valued, visual cues will be developed that express the idea of youth. They might include minimal make-up and clothing that follows body shape in torso with arms and legs exposed.

Since associations of the ABC are usually centered around an important cultural factor, an understanding of these associations means bringing to awareness these cultural factors. If male and female roles are in question in a society, the ABC will be found that reflects this uncertainty. For example, in figure 9.8 a suit form is explored that is identical for males and females—pants for both and jacket tucked in or out.

To interpret the ABC the viewer must ask, What factors are especially impor-

9.8. The ABC is used to explore female and male roles through similar suit forms. *Photo courtesy of Fairchild Visuals, division of Fairchild Publications, Inc., New York City.*

tant to the society? Then, What are the important form images? If exercise and health are valued, examples will be found demonstrating this concern, not only in the forms themselves but in the publicity surrounding them. For example, if exercise and health are believed to be important, look for examples directly related to this value such as jogging suits and new looks in exercise leotards. But you may also discover that the value appears in more general categories of apparel such as casual clothing, as when Norma Kamali expanded the use of cotton knits previously used primarily in sweatsuits. Thus the value may be more pervasive than is initially apparent.

In any social group related approaches emerge for visual forms. For a person who identifies with a particular ABC there may be much more individuality within the identifying characteristics than for an outsider. To communicate through the ABC involves a shared identification within a social group as well as a degree of individual variation within the social reference. This shared identification can be a single item such as beads around the neck or involve the whole ABC as in the white, two-piece costume of the student of karate, with the focus on the color of the belt.

Identifying features can be subtle, only identifiable to the social group sharing them, or very visible and obvious to anyone within or outside the group. How obvious the identifying features are can depend upon how knowing the audience, the viewers of the ABC. For example, to some who wear designer clothing, the success of the experience is dependent upon someone in his or her audience recognizing the designer's stamp, the definers and modifiers combined that season.

Established usages are never completely definite or rigid. Sometimes meanings are ambiguous and situation or event must be considered to determine which meaning is intended. Sometimes if the form is vague in its message, the context of use provides the interpretation. A difficulty in interpretation results from sensory details and individual ABCs taking on different meanings given new situations. New meanings are constantly appearing in a culture and old symbols may take on a new meaning.

TIME MILIEU. Timeliness of visual form of the ABC is called fashion. Fashion is a very influential factor within many cultural groups and can greatly affect perception. There is a dynamic involved in this relation to time because the image may be in a slow but constant state of flux, even though the ABC has some constant patterns. There is consistency amid the change, which is part of a progressive succession of interconnected ideas. A shirtwaist may be more or less in fashion at any one time, but as it dips in and out of fashion, its form may change somewhat.

An apparel category may be enduring, with the associated features changing somewhat with time (fig. 9.9). The term *traditional* can bring to mind a system of associated features, some of them changing over time, but overall the form can remain quite enduring. The identifying features, in this instance, are use of symmetry, small-scale geometric pattern, closed silhouette, close gradations of color within a whole that includes a definite ordering of parts. At any one time the traditional ABC may be fashionable for many within a group or for only a few.

The audience for timely forms also varies. The focus of a youth group may be quite different from that of an older group. Within two groups the criteria of timeliness can be different. However, fashion is seen from different frames of viewing reference. For example, the au-

a   b

9.9. An apparel form such as a classic suit endures with modified features. **a.** *Photo courtesy of Division of Costume, The National Museum of American History, Smithsonian Institution.* **b.** *Photo courtesy of Neiman-Marcus; photographer, Greg Booth.*

dience may have to adjust their observation from reference to the edge of silhouette to surface texture or color. The audience must keep abreast of changes in viewing reference or they will no longer be current.

During any one fashion season different forms with different looks are described. These may be publicized as single-feature orientations or whole expressive patterns. Single-feature emphases are useful because they indicate ABCs are being compared and a message related to one association among them is stressed. Examples include: Color is this season's message; It's all about shape. This approach has the effect of allowing focus on and interpretation of that feature within an ABC. Another category of terms used is that of expressive patterns such as sensuous, sweet, confident. These refer to com-

binations of form properties of the ABC. For example, *confident* may describe in an ABC a combination of strong and calm in expressive effect. Whole expressive effects are often publicized, for example, country casual, romantic, nautical, safari. These wholistic effects are often associated with one or just a few designers, as one message in the total fashion picture.

Time may permeate every aspect of the ABC if newness is an important cultural factor. Apparent newness may include such single features as the worn look of the surface, associated features reflecting the manner in which parts are put together, i.e., the way a blazer is worn, collar up and sleeves pushed up, with a two-piece separate part look, or a one-piece look of top and bottom and more conventional contrasting shirt and tie. Thus fashion involves the entire

9 / Interpreting the ABC: associations of meaning   **145**

9.10. These forms are similar through time but associated meanings change. **a.** *Photo courtesy of Fairchild Visuals, division of Fairchild Publications, Inc., New York City.* **b.** *Photo courtesy of Division of Costume, The National Museum of American History, Smithsonian Institution.*

ABC, the wearing and shaping of hair, the application of cosmetics, body movements. At any one time, the influence of time pervades all aspects of the ABC, requiring the viewer to be comprehensive and flexible.

The recognition of time relations includes past, present, and future, therefore we may use such terms as *historic, up-to-date,* and *space-age.* We describe an old-fashioned girl or a "thoroughly modern Millie." Figure 9.10 illustrates similar forms, one considered historic

and male and one considered modern and female.

Time affects many facets of the ABC, such as the change of the body from youthful to mature. When the youthful look is superimposed upon the effects of aging, the representation of youth may be altered. For example, what is considered youthful at a young age, e.g., body exposure, would have to be altered for an older body. Then youth could be translated as a well-groomed body, well-fitted shapes, and up-to-date colors.

When the youthful look becomes a fashion, if it is to be adopted by many, the form must be translatable to many different groups. Thus, the specific form may take on variations within the unifying idea of youth.

EVENT MILIEU. The specific event at which an ABC is viewed affects the visual form as well as our expectancies of that form. The event may involve certain anticipated features and combinations of features. What is worn in a place of business is different from what is worn socially and our expectancies for each can vary. Consider such terms as *night dressing, sportswear, business suit.* Each term relates to a general or specific event associated with the ABC. Close your eyes and imagine forms of the ABC that associate with a particular event. How specific can you make your image of the ABC for each event? Does one image come to you or several?

Often what we wear depends upon many factors of event—location (town, region of the country), weather, season, and place (theater, restaurant, racquet club), mode of transport, companions, number participating, our mood in anticipation of the event.

The visual form of the ABC may be very location specific, as for example, what visual forms are being worn this year for the Central High School prom in Wobegon, Minnesota. The associated features acceptable for this event may be a relatively loose set or very restrictive. Expectations for prom attire may become more form specific as those planning to attend communicate before the event and establish expectancies.

Regional patterns of dress influence our perceptions. When we plan to travel to a new region for which we have no previous experience but are aware of different weather patterns, we often ask others who have traveled to or lived in that region. We may adapt our present wardrobe to the region or even buy some new forms in anticipation of the travel.

When we begin to anticipate spring, we watch not only for its signs on the landscape but also its forms of ABCs. Viewers have expectations of ABCs that relate to season, especially in regions with definite seasonal patterns. Even though we may accept many ABCs that cross over to another season, we often adopt new forms specific to the season.

What activities and events that we have experienced also affect our expectations of the ABC? We can often think of different expectations to accompany different versions of the same general activity—whether we eat pizza or cordon bleu, whether we attend a movie or live theater, whether we attend this meeting or that one. Who we go with influences our expectations, whether we go alone or with a group. For example, an individual in a group will often dress to match other group members rather than strictly match the event.

SINGLE-EVENT FORMS OR MULTIPLE-EVENT FORMS. The form may be considered to have inherent event features, such as when we describe an ABC as formal or casual. For example, white tie and tails signifies a category of formal event. The suitability of an ABC can vary from being very event specific to being event nonspecific or multiple event. Some forms are more single event, while others are more versatile, i.e., a bride in a wedding dress represents a singular-event form as does a drum major in a marching band costume. Casual summer dress often is multiple event.

The expectancies associated with event are in a constant state of flux. Time and experience change our expectancies. What we consider appropriate in a given situation depends upon what we have experienced in the past. If we have much experience in a given situation, we feel more confident; we know the expected image patterns of appearance and can either choose to match them or vary them somewhat. If, on the other hand, we are entering a new situation, we may choose a conventional multiple-event form.

Time often influences viewing, especially in expectancies of multiple-event forms. At one time an acceptable multiple-event form will be designer blue jeans, a white shirt, and tweed blazer. At another time this form may appear time specific or dated as a multiple-event form, with some other form taking its place.

When an individual quits updating her or his event form, the ABC presented can become very time specific. Often the time-specific, frozen ABC reveals the last time an individual paid any attention to image. Readers of fashion magazines are often fascinated with make-overs, which explicitly reveal what it takes to update an image.

Which events of your acquaintance require single-event forms and which, multiple-event forms? A formal wedding would require single-event forms for the members of the wedding party. On the other hand, many different ABCs could be worn to a large grocery store in a large city. At such a grocery store, what expectations would there be for visual form?

ATTENTION EXPECTANCIES. The role an ABC plays in an event will influence how much attention it receives. If a person is attending a wedding as the bride or groom, expectations for viewer focus would be greater than if attending as an invited guest.

What forms attract more attention? What would allow a participant to fade into the background? The dichotomy between focus and fading into the background varies. An ABC that fades into the background in one situation may stand out in another. For an event at which multiple-event forms are expected, the single-event form may attract attention.

Form associations are specific to the situational milieu of culture, time, and event. Red can mean stop or refer to a holiday, depending upon situation of viewing; red, white, and blue can be associated with patriotism or with spring fashion. As we experience specific situations, we must consider their influence upon the specific expectations accompanying the ABC.

Visual exercises

I. Interpreting the ABC.
   A. Study the ABCs for a fashion season. Examine written comments about the season in the editorial section of a magazine. Then find visual examples of what the writer's verbal description meant. Are there notable aspects of the ABCs the writer ignored or missed in making his or her point? How does an editor present a message?
   B. If possible, use a series of ABCs designed by one individual. Interpret each as to what it means. Ask the designer what he or she intended. Compare your interpretations with the designer's. Are they similar or different? Do both sets of interpretations make sense? What in the ABCs could have caused differences in interpretation?

II. Viewing a fashion show or exhibit.
   A. Attend a fashion show or exhibit and then respond to the following questions.
   B. What showing did you attend? Indicate place, time, etc. Include any program materials you received.
   C. What do you believe was the overall message of the show? Who was the target audience? Why? If you were a

news reporter describing the show, what five adjectives would you use? Summarize the main images.

D. Select one ABC you believe could become widely adopted in the area where you live. Why do you believe this could happen?

E. Describe in detail two specific ABCs you found to be very different visually from each other. A rough sketch could help in the description. Why were they different? Include uses of lines, shapes, colors, textures. What is the part-whole relation? What words would you use to interpret the ABCs? Explain how these ABCs relate to mainstream fashion.

III. Examining predictability and surprise in the ABC.

A. Within one magazine, look for examples of ABCs where surprise influences your initial response.

B. In each ABC what was the reason for the surprise? What are the predictable visual relations within each ABC?

C. Compare the ABCs. Is there a pattern in your response? Is there a similar reason for your surprise in more than one of the ABCs? Is there a similar reason for predictability in more than one of the ABCs?

IV. The ABC and event expectation.

A. Working in groups of three to five, select an event that you have all experienced more than once. Either attend the event or imagine various ABCs at the event.

B. Individually develop a list of attributes of the ABC (definers, organizing factors) (1) that you would expect to find at the event and (2) that would surprise the viewer.

V. Interpreting visual effect.

A. Choose an ABC you have designed or put together as an ensemble.

B. What visual effect did you intend? Try to be specific in describing both the form itself and the intended message.

C. Ask another person what message he or she received. Compare your intention with the other person's response.

VI. Interpreting visual effect.

A. Select a photo of an ABC from a magazine or newspaper.

B. Analyze the ABC and then list words or short phrases that describe its form and message for you.

C. Go through your responses and indicate the nature of each. Is it more individual or universal?

VII. Meaning conveyed through the ABC.

The ABC communicates information to observers. Most of us use this information either consciously or unconsciously when planning what to wear for ourselves or others. Fashion, events, or situations may influence what types of appearance are appropriate. Whether or not messages are being communicated by the ABC within a social group depends upon the degree of shared meaning. The purpose of this exercise is to think about visual characteristics of the ABC within a communication framework.

A. You will be given a word that can describe the effect of the ABC.[1] Consider what that term brings to mind. Imagine an ABC that would be described by the word. Work individually in B and C. In D, share responses with those working on the same term.

B. Answer the following questions according to the term you have been given.

1. Do you imagine this ABC as closed or open, whole-oriented or part-oriented, planar integrated or segregated, flat or rounded, determinate or indeterminate?

2. Describe any features of the body (e.g., height, dark hair) that would reinforce the term or its message.

3. Are there any aspects of the lines and shapes (e.g., square shoulders, trousers, ruffles, soft edges) that would convey this message? Describe.

4. What type of surfaces (i.e., color and texture) would convey this

---

1. *Teacher note:* Assign class members into groups of 4–6. Give each group a term such as youthful, elegant, masculine, feminine, casual, formal, business, pleasure.

message best? What part of the ensemble (upper torso, lower torso, whole body) would each of these surfaces be used for?

5. Describe the interaction of the visual parts. Is there a strong contrast between them? What produces the contrast—value difference, shape variation? Is there an integration between parts? What produces it?

6. Are there any aspects of this visual description you think are most important in conveying this message? What are they?

C.

1. Choose an ABC of which your first impression is the message you just described.

2. Does the ABC you selected differ from the image you described in B? Explain.

D.

1. Get together with those working on the same term and note differences and similarities of responses.

2. Discuss the ways in which an ABC can communicate a message. How much detail is needed to discriminate between similar ABCs?

3. Summarize your discussion and record it. Be ready to turn in descriptions and/or share with the class.

10

The expert viewer: professional considerations

THE systematic approach to appraising ABCs introduced in this book offers a method of educating oneself beyond personal intuition. This approach encourages the development of skills that will lead to a more complete understanding of the ABC. This skill development requires patience and a continuing use of the approach in order to develop perceptual skills to the fullest. In this chapter the framework for analysis will be restated incorporating the language that is the foundation for expanding viewing capabilities.

The professional's role

What about the professional applications of the systematic approach? After educating oneself beyond personal intuition, the expert viewer has acquired the skills necessary to be objective. A professional can apply such knowledge and skills for a particular client. But the professional must also understand the client's viewpoint, which may be that of the casual observer. The client, broadly conceived, is any individual or group who has an interest in achieving a particular goal. This could be a customer, a store staff, or a magazine staff with whom the professional must interact.

The expert viewer has a comprehensive view of the ABC and has developed an ability to understand and then control the visual effect. He or she can become the interpreter of the ABC to the client. The professional is able to evaluate effectiveness based upon some specific criteria, either the client's objectives or an expanded version of them. A client may communicate image objectives but not know how to achieve them. A store may need an estimate of how important a specific item of apparel will be this season; a magazine may need a written interpretation of a local fashion event.

Many clients know when a result is effective and can make subjective judgments about the result, but they don't know, or need to know, the steps in between (see fig. 1.2). That is the job of the expert viewer who chooses to apply the knowledge to a profession. For example, a client can see the difference between a determinate, closed, viewed-as-a-whole ABC and its opposite. Though expressing a judgment about the visual result, the client does not necessarily want to, or need to, know what caused the visual difference. Thus working directly through visual images is an effective way to communicate with a client.

The professional needs to understand the point of view of the client. This means developing an ability to interpret a client's objectives, to take the client's stated intentions and expand and interpret them in visual form.

An expert viewer's framework

Adopting a systematic approach is necessary to the development of the perceptual skills that lead to a more discriminating response. The expert viewer has learned to identify and describe the specifics of an ABC through a systematic process. An objective language documents perception of the form. The process includes observation of the ABC within its spatial parameters documented by polar word pairs. Analysis of the form includes observation of the structure of the body and its materials, definers, and modifiers and their influence on organization. Interpretation and evaluation follow the observation and analysis and are the more subjective aspects of the approach. But the viewer brings to the final interpretation and evaluation an expanded contextual framework. What follows is a restatement of the steps developed in chapter 2, incorporating the language introduced in chapters 2–9.

STEPS IN THE PERCEPTUAL PROCESS

1. Observation: Attending to and describing what we see
   a. Note existing descriptive information for help in understanding the form. This includes such information as designer, manufacturer, date of creation or display, country of origin, for whom intended, materials and techniques used.
   b. Focus on the entire form. (Refer to chaps. 3, 4, 5, and 6 for discussion.) Observe and describe what is there as completely as possible. How is the silhouette defined? How does the form separate from the surrounding space? Is it *closed* or *open, whole* or *part*? What is *figure* and what is *ground*? Are the surfaces *flat* or *rounded, determinate* or *indeterminate*?
   c. Describe the features that define the form. How is the body defined? What is emphasized and what has priority—*body* or *clothing*? What type of *structuring* is used—layout, surface, and/or shadow?
      What *linear definers* are used? What types of points, lines, shapes? Are they rounded, angular, or straight? How many are there? What is their orientation—vertical, horizontal, or diagonal? Size—small or large? What are the *surface definers*? What types of colors are used? Describe each color as to hue, value, and intensity. What textures are used? Are they rough or smooth, crisp or soft? How do light and shadow affect the surface?
2. Analysis: Consider the relations in what we see
   In this step the influence of one part on another is analyzed. (Refer especially to chaps. 6, 7, and 8.)
   a. Order the parts. Which parts are noticed first? Number the parts in the order in which they are viewed.
   b. Examine the parts within the whole in further detail. Why were you attracted first to part number 1, then 2, and then 3? What separates from the whole for attention? How many separate parts are there? How are the parts modified within the whole? What influence do definers have? Consider *Gestalt principles of organization: similarity, closure, proximity, continuation.* Explain the significance of the modifiers—*number, direction, visual weight, size, spatial position.*
   c. Describe *organization.* Is the eye directed throughout the form? If directed is it vertical, horizontal,

or circular? What causes the direction of the visual path? If undirected, are the parts separate and independent? What is *grouping* and what is *separating*? What part was the point of entry? How does it become a source of focus? Which parts refer the viewer to the whole ABC?

3. Interpretation: What summarizes the form?

At this stage, look for the associations of form and meaning that seem to summarize and explain the form. This step builds upon the above two. (See chaps. 8 and 9 for discussion.)

a. Note whether the ABC encourages *simultaneous* viewing of the whole, *successive,* or *separated.* How much activity is taking place? How many relationships are there? What are the priority relationships?

b. Consider and record all associations. At first record them without judgment. Consider all alternatives of interpretation. Pull from all past experiences, consider and test alternatives of interpretation.

What associations are directly observed in the form? Step back from the evidence provided by direct observation and consider indirect associations. What within the ABC relates to cultural values and priorities? What would interest viewers? How does the ABC relate to specific situations?

c. Select the *ideas* that help to *characterize* the ABC. Consider your first impressions from b. Which seem to be possible and probable? To what audience(s) might the ABC appeal? What are the features forming your impressions? Are they different from those you originally thought were the controlling features? Consider

how the ABC is organized and how its ideas are presented.

4. Evaluation: Developing a critique

Evaluation is the final step of the perceptual process. By this time the viewer is assured that evaluation will be more objective because it follows the previous three steps. To evaluate an ABC means to be continually aware of the criteria we use in the process. They identify our orientation to the ABC. A set of criteria helps us see more and learn more from our viewing. At the beginning of this book, the casual viewer was urged to suspend subjective judgment in order to become an educated viewer. However, subjectivity does have a place in evaluation.

Evaluation can range from that with a degree of objectivity to that with total subjectivity. Consider the difference. A subjective evaluative response is an expression of an individual's unique point of view. An example would be, "I love red! Once I had a red shirt and it always gave me a good feeling when I wore it."

A more objective evaluative response involves a knowledge of culturally established expectations, such as, "Red, white, and blue are colors worn together this spring." This comment could come from an observer who is making an objective observation based upon collective agreement. Personal attitudes are purposely kept separate from the evaluation.

Evaluation is more than knowing what we think is good or bad. Our "wow" needs backing up with reason. This means being aware of personal judgment and differentiating between that and what is universal, for example, "The color of the ABC could be attractive to many viewers, although it would not be a personal choice."

A viewer who uses her or his own experiences and point of view to observe and evaluate can develop an awareness of a more universal point of view. To ignore personal feelings is to bypass a potentially valuable source of associations. An educated viewer who is aware of personal response can test it against others' responses. Then he or she can choose to separate or include the personal response in an evaluation. In this way a viewer can expand a point of view and even move toward understanding a more universal response.

CRITERIA FOR EVALUATION. Evaluation can focus primarily on the form, the viewer, or the situation. The viewer who is aware of the different foci can began to differentiate evaluative criteria.

THE FORM OF THE ABC. When the focus is on the form itself, the viewer may conclude that the form is interesting to look at and that this is enough evaluation. A pertinent question could be, Is it particularly interesting as a visual form because of the many viewing relationships? An ABC with more than one visual linkage of parts to whole can actively involve the viewer with the form. This process can be satisfying for the viewer who has educated him or herself to flexible viewing of multiple relationships.

Fashion writers often describe clothing as a good background piece or a good focus. Such a description derives from what is viewed as figure and what is ground. What other purposes could the ABC fulfill visually? How is an ABC characterized? Expressive effects can arise out of the sensations of viewing the ABC. In chapter 9 expressive effects were associated with certain combinations of form properties and included exciting, calm, delicate, and strong. Expressions can influence the visual effect.

The degree of "newness," the element of surprise as it relates to each ABC, is what is often noticed. However, timeliness also has a degree of consistency. Certain properties can be identified as gradually changing. In other words the message changes gradually and relates to a particular width of lapel or length of hem or it changes from one definer to another, e.g., this year color, next year shape or texture. Sometimes fashion is identified by an entire look, as the Gunne Sax look or the 1947 New Look. Thus the ABC is continually changing, and the ABC that was so delightful to look at yesterday is too predictable today.

"Worth the investment" is a phrase we often hear in an evaluation of the form. Marketplace cost, purpose, and durability are used as guides for evaluation; e.g., it is expensive so it must be good; it is good enough for the intended purpose; it is a good buy because it will only be worn once or twice or it will last for a long time and through many wearings. Finally wearing such apparel may give the owner viewing pleasure or status. Thus the evaluation of the form is combined with purpose and cost.

SITUATION—TIME, CULTURE, EVENT. When focus is upon situation, that is, time, culture, and event, the viewer might consider the form in terms of fashion. In what way is the ABC predictable? What about it is new? To answer these questions the viewer needs to consider what has come before and what may follow. How is the form a product of its time? How is it similar to other ABCs of the time? What will follow? If the ABC needs to be considered as a product of the time, is it a creator of timeliness, i.e., is the ABC of value because it points the way to new forms? Or is it a classic piece that fulfills or even exceeds our expectations in its combination of materials, colors, lines, or shapes?

Does the form extend or intensify the cultural values of its audience, that is, both users and viewers? What happens if the form communicates a message to which the viewer objects? The ABC can communicate simple congruous messages as well as complex and incongruous messages. For what purposes might we require an ABC to be congruous in its message? For what purposes might we stress the incongruous or the unexpected?

Events often are linked to expected image patterns of the ABC. When we use the terms *casual* or *formal* in reference to an ABC, we are relating to event. The relation of an ABC to an event is a common source of evaluation and occurs when we respond to an ABC by asking, "But where could this be worn?" "Is it appropriate for this event?" We are viewing with an image before us.

AUDIENCE. Evaluation often centers around the general audience for the form—those likely to appreciate it. How many could or would be wearers? Who would be interested in viewing the ABC? Few viewers? Many viewers?

What is the appeal of the ABC to satisfy the unique-to-me needs of specific people, the collective needs of many?

Designers and manufacturers often have an audience in mind as they work. An evaluation could then be centered on their intentions related to the particular form. Thus knowing the origin aids in understanding the form. Designers and manufacturers are often consistent in their approach and their ABCs evolve over time. The form can be evaluated for its consistency, that is, whether the designer has changed direction and is appealing to a different audience.

Understanding the casual viewer

In chapter 1 a type of perceptual filter was discussed, viewing habit. The idea was that we miss many of the nuances of the ABC if we rely too much on past habits of viewing. At that time the observer was being asked to expand viewing to understand the visual effect of the ABC. But consider habit from another point of view—the need to realize how the casual observer is likely to attend to the ABC and the way in which this awareness can help establish a professional relation with a client.

Casual viewers often see the ABC through a perceptual filter. Selective attention is the use of a point of view that filters perception through a system of recognizable associations—a mental set of expectations that the viewer adopts in perceiving an ABC. The expert viewer needs to understand the perceptual filter of the casual viewer, who may become a client. Some attributes of the ABC become more important when a particular perceptual filter is established. Only one or two attributes may be constant and important in a filter. Thus, if the salience of a client's expectations is known, the professional can be more precise in meeting those expectations.

The casual observer's attention is always selective, noticing some things and ignoring others. Since the casual observer does not usually spend the time required to understand the ABC thoroughly, he or she will adopt a point of view that leads to the desired result. For example, when looking for clothing for camping, a particular filter may be adopted, one emphasizing the protective attributes of the clothing based on past camping experiences.

Viewing filters can be utilized to measure any given ABC with a viewer's expectations. What expectations can an observer utilize in selective perception?

Some of the sources of association to the ABC that can influence an observer's selective attention can be identified. For example, if we want to find an ABC that is fashionable, we may filter out everything unfashionable. Consider how responses to the ABC would change based upon adoption of one or more of the following filters.

SENSORY EXPERIENCES. Our direct sensory experiences affect us and influence our expectations. Our sensory experiences—visual, tactile, kinesthetic, auditory, and olfactory—are a source of filter in the ABC. For example, an observer who gives a compliment on a particular article of clothing often requires a tactile reinforcement. "My, what a lovely shirt. May I touch it?" Confirmation is made by rubbing the surface of the shirt sleeve between the fingers.

Meaning arises from active exploration of our physical environment. Very early in life we learn from pushing, pulling, and touching objects. We are influenced by the tactile experiences of early childhood, the slipperiness of the ribbon on the binding of a blanket, the softness of a teddy bear, the pleasure of being rubbed dry with a towel, or the sensation of a mother's hair brushing against us.

Early sensory experiences can carry over into other experiences that relate the tactile and visual. A visual preference for rich or deep colors may be the result of previous pleasant tactile experiences. An observer who particularly enjoys color is sensuously involved in the visual aspects of the surfaces of materials. So too is the observer who likes primarily visual textural effects; a tweed coat is often more interesting to look at than to touch. A plaid surface also is primarily a visual experience, athough an observer will sometimes run a hand over the surface anyway.

Auditory and olfactory responses are less directly related to visual response but still may be influential in certain instances. Think of the effect of the swish or crackle of a crisp taffeta skirt or the marching sound of heels clicking against a sidewalk. Does the sound in any way affect other senses? The scent of perfume as a person walks toward us is a direct sensory experience. Can smell affect our visual experience of the ABC? Yes it can!

FAMILIARITY WITH NATURAL OBJECTS. Satisfying past experiences are an important part of expectancies. We continually look for the familiar as a source of satisfying visual experiences. A viewing filter may develop based upon the resemblance of the form to natural objects. The viewer responds to the ABC based upon the degree to which it resembles natural forms.

There are many examples where reference is made to objects of nature. We often use terms such as *earth colors, wheat,* or *cornflower blue.* We even refer to fibers giving a "natural" look. We associate various shapes with natural objects; we compare surface motifs for their resemblance to natural objects. We describe floral shapes as *realistic* or *abstracted* and *stylized.* Many realistic shapes have been knitted into sweaters, and shapes resembling leaves are used in jewelry and on handbags.

TRADITION. We often respond to the ABC based upon tried-and-true formulas. The successful effects get repeated. The term *classic* when applied to clothing can refer to visual forms recognized as exemplary in the past. We then respond to their continued use with the pleasure of recognition.

Tradition can be applied to any of the single form properties or a combination. For example, use of the colors red, white, and blue is considered traditional and visually effective. Such traditional colors can be variously applied to the ABC and create quite different visual effects. However, in a perceptual filter the different visual uses are not so much noticed as is the formula.

This perceptual filter can apply to whole ABCs. For example, the Chanel suit varies somewhat from ABC to ABC, but the overall form has become traditional—the use of colorful surfaces visually textured with braid outlining the shapes of the collarless cardigan suit jacket.

PREFERENCES. All things considered, preference is a most influential viewing filter. Preferences can come from sensory experiences with the ABC and be expressed when we are choosing among alternatives. But preferences can arise out of experiences having less to do with the form than with our motive. For example, we may prefer a particular ABC based upon a need to belong in a group or to deny the values of a group. Regardless of the motive, an understanding of our preferences will help us better understand our visual response to an ABC.

Our preferences usually relate to structural combinations of edges and surfaces as well as to associations to life events and to what we value. Often we like something because we can identify with it. We react to the world with an affinity for some things and a revulsion toward others. This could include a fondness for a certain combination of colors because we always get compliments on them or a liking of a slim and vibrant appearing image because this is the way we want to look. Our reactions result in formation of preferences expressed in comments such as "I like this," "This gives me pleasure," "That is so ugly!"

Our preferences are generalized expressions of our likes or dislikes. The formation of patterns of what we like and dislike can be the ultimate influence on our evaluative response. Preferences are influenced by others of our social group, families, friends. Within the context of our social group we develop formal and informal guidelines of use. We view what others are wearing, where and how they are wearing it, and what they are wearing with what. The direction and extent of our visual education can influence preference.

FULFILLMENT OF HUMAN NEEDS. Another primary source of filtering is related to satisfaction of our basic needs. This would include relief of hunger with food, exhaustion with a bed and blankets, cold with a warm sweater or coat. The way clothing can function within a society also includes the satisfaction of higher level needs, such as social or self-actualization. Translated into how we perceive clothing: shoes may look sexy, sweaters warm, trousers comfortable.

In perception the observer may respond visually to the way it appears the ABC could fulfill a basic need. Generalization from our past experiences with apparel helps to establish these expectancies. The ABC is viewed as fulfilling a function in many instances, that is, efficiently satisfying the requirements of intended purpose. The degree to which the ABC satisfies the apparent purpose is related to our perception of its use. For example, we can view a raincoat primarily as to the manner in which it appears it will keep us dry.

PRODUCT CRAFTING. Production of apparel takes technical skill and we often use a term such as *quality* to describe apparel produced with excellent technique. Here is yet another source of filtering. The skill required to put together a particular article of clothing is referred to as good workmanship. As with any perceptual filter, it can become exclusive in our filtering and thus we miss other aspects of visual effect.

Technical skill and workmanship can strongly influence our perception of the ABC. Workmanship can become especially important if traced to an identifiable individual or manufacturer. An observer may respond to the degree of difficulty in constructing clothing because of past personal experience with a technique, tailoring or knitting, for example. However, the observer does not need to have had personal experience to appreciate technical skill. Think of the number of times you hear reference to "shoddy workmanship."

An example of the expectations based upon workmanship is "That is not worth the price—look at how poorly it is made!" Such a statement implies a marketplace standard of technical skill relative to the appearance and the price. There is no doubt that the ABC is affected by the skill taken to produce it. A problem arises only when the filter becomes too pervasive.

Getting to know and understand our own viewing filters helps us to be aware of their priority in our evaluation process. What viewing filters are used? Does a viewing filter change depending upon circumstance? Are there certain filters that always affect perception regardless of what is being viewed? It is possible to change viewing filters unconsciously as we view different ABCs. To educate our vision is to be aware of the specific nature of our viewing expectations.

Evaluative response to the ABC

An evaluative response often involves the filter of expectancies. One or more filters may be used, which, if identified, would help to predict the expectations of a client in his or her perception

of the ABC. This does not mean the professional must yield completely to a client's viewpoint. The professional can work at broadening the viewpoint through verbal illustration or visual display.

When expectancies associated with an ABC are met, a viewer experiences a degree of satisfaction, a fulfillment based upon expectations. However, some expectations are easier to fulfill than others. Expectations of comfort in men's pajamas may be met with a standard pajama on the market. The viewer may not experience a high degree of satisfaction from such easy fulfillment. Expectations that are easily met do not result in the same degree of satisfaction as those that are more difficult to meet.

Expectancies may be ignored in full knowledge of what those expectancies are, as in a joke. We can enjoy such a denial when intended. We can usually recognize when this denial of expectancy is unintended. We may not take seriously a very young girl in a black satin, close-to-the-body dress at a junior prom. She is excused because of her innocence. The message represented by her clothing is too incongruous with the expectations of event as well as with the maturity of her body. She appears to be playing dress-up.

The greatest satisfaction may be in fulfilling difficult expectancies, or going beyond our minimal expectations to excellence when expectancies are less difficult to meet. Thus some ABCs may adequately meet our expectations and others not only meet but exceed them. In this way evaluation is tied to the criteria of expectancy.

Continuing the approach

The viewer who persists in developing perceptual skills using the approach outlined in this book will soon develop enough viewing curiosity to continue the process. Making as complete an analysis as possible will allow the expert viewer to discover many factors that will affect an evaluation of the ABC. The viewer can utilize past experiences and present expectations to evaluate the ABC.

What does it take to understand the ABC? The lesson of being able to look at the whole ABC as a frame of reference is most important. Viewing must be a continual, searching, interactive, two-way process. When an ABC is being viewed, an active viewer continues to question the visual effect.

All of the skills involved in the systematic approach to the ABC cannot be developed simultaneously or understood immediately. For example, while learning to understand color, the observer often ignores shape. But in continuing with the systematic approach, the whole ABC will remain the viewing reference and eventually both color and shape will be understood. The observer needs to keep working on these various skills.

The viewer who learns to understand one ABC, then another, will develop an understanding of a spectrum of forms. As exposure broadens the spectrum, an inventory will develop. The viewer who has become educated will continually have to set new boundaries by extending and filling this range.

As the framework for analysis of one ABC is understood, then comparisons of one form to another can be made. This ability to make comparisons has many uses. The viewer can learn to analyze existing forms for various trends. In the field of fashion apparel new forms are continually offered for viewing consideration. Flexibility in analyzing ABCs will broaden one's viewing and enable perception and interpretation of unfamiliar and new visual experiences. These could be new trends within a culture or a comparison of forms from different cultures.

To understand the ABC over time goes beyond understanding any one of its dimensions, such as color or cut of clothing. The study of change in the ABC should incorporate a study of change in organization. An analysis could involve predictable relations and distinctive features of a particular designer—constancy and change over time.

But what incentives are there to continue? What are the rewards if a viewer introduced to this approach continues to work at developing perceptual skills? There are several possible outcomes.

DEVELOP IMAGINATIVE SKILLS. As a viewer becomes more skilled perceptually, a new understanding of forms and new relationships can be developed. This is especially necessary for the designer. Imaginative powers can be developed because the viewer begins to think in visual terms. The effect of viewer interaction with visual form is important for a professional to understand.

The viewer who learns how properties of form tend to be viewed can begin to think beyond one form, from forms already experienced to forms as yet uncreated. A "what if" attitude helps in developing an ability to visualize or imagine substitutions. First the viewer creates a mental picture of the form as it exists, then tries to imagine what would happen if another color were substituted for the existing one. What would the difference be? What changes in viewing would occur? The viewer who has learned to consider the effects of one color within the ABC can expand to consider the effects of other colors.

The designer needs these skills at several stages. A designer can begin with the raw materials of the ABC and produce apparel from an image by manipulating those materials. At another stage a designer combines separate apparel items. This designer puts images together for presentation or display. He or she could be an interpreter of many visual forms—for example, a store manager or the promotor of the ABC in window displays, fashion shows, layout for advertising copy.

DEVELOP COMMUNICATION SKILLS. Many ABCS are created to influence large numbers of people, to affect how they feel, think, or act. An ABC, thoughtfully planned and developed, can help to set the stage for a festive or serious mood. Image makers know an image can be controlled through appearance to create a friendly, approachable impression or a no-nonsense impression of control. There is much we can communicate with the ABC. Much time and thought can go into the visual effect, as in the case of costumes for movie or theater performances, clothing and cosmetics worn by men and women in public positions. Think of the many fields relating apparel design to communication: theater costume, photography, fashion editor. The ABC is a message carrier and careers are based upon its communicative power.

We have a lot to learn about communication. As we continue to analyze and interpret the ABC, we can understand how many associations are related to clothing. The ABC must be carefully analyzed and interpreted for its general message. If "power dressing" is the goal, then certain ABCs can be utilized; but if an approachable friendly impression is desired, the ABC can set that stage too. One prominent male lecturer takes off his jacket in the first few seconds of a presentation to signify an approachable, "I'm not so serious as I first appear." Another keeps his jacket on to signify, "I am in control here!"

The viewer may better communicate messages of clothing who first applies

the step of interpretation. While this book is not a how-to-dress book, it does offer the wearer a framework for communication of appearance through personal dressing. But the framework goes beyond personal dressing. If this initiation to a visual process is continued, the viewer will progress in viewing skills. Then analysis of dress can extend to a professional concern. The retailer in a fashion-based store can better understand the market. The designer can use systematic analysis in the creative process. The wardrobe consultant can better understand the point of view of clientele.

Visual Exercises

I. Interpreting the message of an ABC.
   A. Select pictures of several ABCs that appear to have a range of meaning associations. Write down what you think each means.
   B. Ask two groups of observers representing different types of viewing reference (e.g., designer, nondesigner; retailer, consumer; young, old; male, female) to write down their impression of the message in what they see.
   C. Compare interpretations. What could have been the basis for each interpretation?

II. Making the familiar, strange.
   A. Select a familiar ABC for consideration.
   B. Pretend you are from another century or another planet. Describe the ABC, being careful not to take anything for granted.

III. Considering the expert's view.
   A. Examine ABCs that an expert critic has said have visual merit. (The expert could be a fashion editor of a magazine or newspaper.) Decide whether you think they have visual merit. Then read the interpretation of the expert.
   B. What criteria were being used by the expert for his or her analysis? Decide whether the expert was referring only to the ABC or to other known factors, such as unusual work of the designer.

IV. Identifying a personal aesthetic: Learning to back up your "wow."

Aesthetics is a term that can be related to the ABC on two levels. Both are important in understanding the ABC. In the broader sense it involves all systematic understanding and reasoning about the ABC. In a more specific and narrower sense it relates to one's judgment of the ABC, that is, the basis on which one decides whether or not the ABC has value. Evaluation is affected by both cultural and individual factors.

If not understood, the more specific aspect of aesthetics can alter and even deter steps taken to improve oneself in the broader aspect. For example, some observers only "see" what they like. To make a judgment does not require us to understand the ABC as a visual form. We develop shorthand methods of acquiring meaning from what we see without really having to take it in. Therefore, a useful exercise is to identify the basis of one's personal aesthetic (the narrower sense).

The following activities can help in the identification of a personal aesthetic.
A. Collect photos of ABCs you both like and dislike.
B. Record what you specifically like or dislike about each photo. Be specific as to visual relations that define visual priorities.
C. Try to generalize: Are there similarities among your likes and dislikes? That is, do you tend to view color or texture with different levels of enjoyment?
D. Summarize B and C by writing the results. Think about to what extent your personal evaluation of the ABC affects what you see.

V. Understanding the steps in the perceptual process.
A. Select and compare two ABCs contrasting in visual effect.
B. Follow the steps in the perceptual process as outlined in this chapter.

Glossary

ABC—apparel-body construct; a visual form that results from interaction of apparel on the human body; a concept of this physical object based upon sensory data

aesthetics—all systematic attempts to understand the viewing of the ABC, evaluation being the end of the process (*see* analytic perception)

analytic perception—process of viewing by four systematic steps: (1) observe, (2) analyze, (3) interpret, (4) evaluate (synonym: systematic analysis)

attending—process by which viewer is engaged in viewing an ABC, involves both attraction and sustained viewing

attraction—means by which viewer is engaged in attending to the ABC

axis—visual reference used to gauge and compare parts. For example, center of ABC may be a vertical reference when sides are treated symmetrically.

blending—possessing a relation of similar visual parts, one part not being dominant over another; characterized by gradual changes resulting from soft edges, similarity of visual surface

body-clothes priority—whether primary viewing focus in ABC is on body or clothes

body form—existing physical structure of trunk, head, and four limbs; component of ABC including body surfaces, all shapes created by body parts, body movements

body surfaces—physical exterior of the body, including textures of skin and hair and colors of skin, hair, and eyes

body view—view of body form from frame of reference of visual field; single viewpoint (front, back, or side)

centering—process of looking for a center point or line upon which activity is focused

characterization—a description of unifying ideas or themes that make a form recognizable, different from other forms

classic—characterized by expected visual pattern, tried-and-true traditional formula

client—a person seeking the advice of a professional

closed—self-contained, continuous, and independent from surround, descriptive of silhouette of ABC

closure—the process of perceiving a grouping or segregating of visual parts, including the connecting of implied lines, to create a bounded area (Gestalt principle of organization)

color—the spectrum of light perception, which provides definition and potential visual relationships through the dimensions of hue, value, and intensity

complexity—the quality of possessing multiple visual relations among parts of an ABC; a situation wherein the parts within the whole are perceived to have several different linkages

context—the visual activity within the ABC, relationship among parts and between parts and whole

continuation—the extension of a visual path by a visual connection between parts (Gestalt principle of organization)

contrast—an abrupt change; a break from similarity and homogeneity; a visual difference that attracts relatively more observer attention

controlling relationship—cause of visual linkage of parts, grouping, and separation of parts, e.g., a definer, a modifier, a Gestalt principle of organization

cool—displaying the visual effect of certain hue variations that produce an impression of distance and of being cold or physically cool, specifically, violet to blue to green; possessing the quality of any color that has been mixed with gray or another cool color

definer—a component of the ABC that produces visual activity; visual details of form, e.g., line, shape, point, color, texture

definition—parameters establishing a particular form; that which creates visual notice (*see* definer)

design—the planning for the structure of a visual form; also, the result of a planning and imaging process

determinate—appearing immediate and definite in the occupation of space, descriptive of surfaces of ABC; possessing either clear-cut level of figure to ground or little to no separation into levels of figure-ground

direction—viewer's impression of movement while taking in the ABC

discontinuous—characterized by abruptly changing direction

edge—line that identifies a bounded area

entirety—a discrete visual entity, the whole ABC

event—an occasion; an occurrence that marks a viewer's time frame. Factors of event are location, season, activity.

expectancies—expectations the viewer brings to the viewing process as a result of past experiences; anticipation by viewer of that which she/he considers the norm

expectancy fulfillment—satisfaction of expectancies

expert viewer—a person trained to view ABCs systematically; one who perceives and understands the visual relations present in a visual form

expressive effect—a unifying idea that summarizes an ABC; a fusion of meaning that arises from emotional states, e.g., excitement, calmness, strength, delicacy

figure—that which we view as having object quality, appears to be in front of ground

figure-ground—an expression of the relations of a form in space in terms of fore- and background; a degree of apparent projection of visual units from a frame of reference, e.g., silhouette or surface. Figure appears in front of ground.

figure-ground ambiguity—a viewing situation in which reversals can occur in what appears as figure, i.e., that which at one time appears as figure switches and becomes ground

filter—a specific purpose that influences viewing; viewer expectancies that shorten the viewing process, utilizing selective attention

flat—appearing primarily as a two-dimensional planar surface

focus—a viewing center; process by which a viewer fixates on a portion of a visual field; a concentration of visual activity that contrasts to some degree with adjacent space

Gestalt principles of organization—four primary principles—similarity, closure, proximity, continuation—that explain the grouping and separating of visual parts in the viewing process (*see* grouping; segregating)

Gestalt psychologists—psychologists who concluded that the process of organizing a discrete entity (a whole) is interactive and automatic

gradation—a measurable variation of some attribute within a whole; a gradual progression of difference that provides visual direction

ground—the field of visual activity of an ABC; that which surrounds and appears to lie beneath figure

grouping—the process of relating similar visual units in perception, an automatic, interactive viewer process that helps in understanding organization of ABC when brought to consciousness

hand—manipulative potential of materials of the ABC, includes weight and drape; tactile qualities of materials

hue—the spectrum variation of color

imaging—creating a visual image in the mind; calling to mind a previous ABC or expected viewing pattern

implied lines—two points of interest connected by viewer

indeterminate—appearing thick or indefinite and blurred in the occupation of space, descriptive of surfaces of ABC; perceived as filled space as a result of visual texture or incorporation of light and shadow

integration—a sense of consistency achieved by dispersing activity within the ABC; similarity of visual parts causing visual interdependence

intensity—strength of pigmentation or degree of purity of a color

interpretation—a summary of the visual effect of the ABC; the third step in a systematic analysis

kinesthetic—sensing position and movement of body through nerve ends

layout structuring—the arrangement of the ABC by three-dimensional means such as shaping by seams, draping, pleats, gathers; manipulations of physical surfaces toward and away from observer and sometimes the three-dimensional effect of surface protrusions

line—actual or imagined linkages between points or areas; a contour

linear definition—the characterization of line and edge in the ABC; visual appearance derived from line and shape

matte surface—a surface with a dull finish

meaning—the sense made of what is viewed, a result of a specific visual structure's effect upon the viewer; a naming process based upon categories of wearing or use and resulting from interaction of viewer with form and situation; interpretation, e.g., expressive effect or evaluation of an ABC

message congruity—a situation in which visual relations match expectancies; similar characterization in the parts of an ABC

mileu—surroundings; situation of viewing of ABC

modifiers—factors that affect the interaction of visual parts of ABC, i.e., size, number, spatial position, direction, and visual weight

movement—a viewing path taken by an observer based upon a comparison of visual relations

multiple-event form—an ABC meant for a variety of occasions; form possessing situation versatility

number—a modifier of the ABC, quantity of a given part within a whole

open—indistinct and interdependent with surround, descriptive of silhouette of ABC

ordinary perception—casual or subjective viewing that relies on immediate identification and visual filtering, not systematic or analytic

organization—structure of visual form; arrangement of visual parts within a whole

organizing—the process of grouping and separating within the context of an ABC

parts—units of visual perception that achieve some measure of distinctness or separation from surround

part-to-whole—characterized by an initial separation of and emphasis on units smaller than the whole

path—direction taken while scanning the ABC; a linkage between two foci

perceptible—viewed directly as a result of the sensory system

pigment—coloring matter

planar—appearing to be on a flat surface parallel to the visual field

planar integration—a viewing situation in which figure appears on a plane very close to ground

planar separation—a viewing situation in which figure appears to be on a plane at some distance from its ground

planar viewing—viewing the ABC as one or a series of surfaces parallel to the observer

plane—a defined, flat or level surface

point—the dot in perception; the intersection of two or more lines; a source of focus when single and strong

preferences—generalized expression of viewer likes and dislikes

professional—an expert viewer who can apply concepts based upon knowledge of the ABC and therefore aid a client

proportion—size relations of parts to each other and to the whole

proximity—similarity of location or close spatial placement of parts. As the distance between like units varies, those that are close spatially will tend to group; those that are distant tend to separate. (Gestalt principle of organization)

reflecting surface—a surface that allows for variation in light and shadow; one that throws back light

rounded—appearing as a three-dimensional, cylindrical surface

scanning—process by which viewer surveys the space of the ABC or the visual field

segregating—visually separating unlike units from the whole ABC, an automatic process of the viewer when parts are visually different

sensory data—information taken in directly through senses, i.e., visual, tactile, kinesthetic, auditory, and olfactory

sensory scheme—visual relations of ABC that are the result of viewer comparing similarities and differences among definers and modifiers

separated—characterized by visually equal and independent parts that are perceived first in a pattern of organization

shadow structuring—means of arranging the ABC by varying light and shadow effects

shape—a bounded area usually perceived as having at least the two dimensions of length and width (planar) or three dimensions by including depth (that which appears thick and rounding)

silhouette—the outline of the ABC, defining the extent of the form distinctly or indistinctly (see closed; open)

similarity—the relative degree of sameness among visual parts that determines their perceptual connection. Parts that are similar tend to be organized into groups by the observer; parts that are different tend to be viewed separately. (Gestalt principle of organization)

simultaneous—being perceived as a whole first in a pattern of organization because of blending surfaces, overall surface treatment, or a closed silhouette

single-event form—an ABC meant for one occasion, e.g., a wedding or christening gown

situation—circumstance of viewing the ABC; includes immediate surround as well as broader influences of time, culture, and event

size—variable of parts in terms of area occupied; a factor that affects visual weight

space of ABC—area of the visual form, including ABC itself, immediately adjacent surround, and area between form and viewer

spatial position—actual or apparent location of ABC relative to the observer and of parts relative to the whole

structure—source of organization or arrangement of visual parts within context of the whole, especially of those form features that direct movement

structuring—processes of constructing or manipulating the ABC; visual form relations achieved by layout, surface, light and shadow

style—a distinctive form structure, consistent and recognizable over time; visual effect that includes form relations and expressive effect

subtlety—an aspect of an ABC not readily perceived by the viewer

successive—characterized by a hierarchy of visual parts, primary and secondary foci

surface definition—the way in which surfaces of the ABC are characterized by texture and color

surface structuring—the arrangement of the ABC by two-dimensional means, e.g., printing, weaving, color variation of materials, that may result in a three-dimensional appearance.

surround—space immediately around the ABC and between ABC and viewer

systematic analysis—an approach to viewing by an investigative, interactive process that consists of four parts: (1) observe, (2) analyze, (3) interpret, (4) evaluate (synonym: analytic perception)

tactile—referring to the sense of touch; perceived by touch

textured—having a surface that appears filled and active, often from weaving or printing

transition—a connection occurring when a part functions to relate two visually stronger parts

value—the degree of lightness or darkness of a color

viewer—one who views, bringing to the viewing process the combined influences of slowly changing traits such as education and personality and rapidly changing traits such as moods and momentary expectations

viewing pattern—order in which the ABC is viewed

viewing priority—that which attracts viewer attention first; that which is perceived as dominant in the visual field, related to its strength and amount of visual activity

viewing tempo—rate at which the viewer perceives the ABC, dependent on amount and type of activity and resulting effect on the viewer

visual field—the physical space around one from his/her stationary point of view (changes according to viewer position)

visual levels—the appearance of an ABC in which surfaces are separated into figure and ground

visual relations—influence of one part upon another or upon the whole; similarities and differences among visual parts within an ABC

visual response—behavioral outcome of three-way interaction of form, situation of viewing, and viewer

visual texture—surface variations of the ABC, perceived not as individual units but rather as multiple, tiny constants dispersed on a surface

visual weight—a modifier of the ABC, visual importance or interest level of a given part when compared to other parts

visual world—a view of the physical space around us as unbounded, resulting in the appearance of constancy in object attributes (involves reliance on past viewing experiences to interpret constancy)

warm—displaying the visual effect of certain hue variations that produce an impression of closeness and of heat, specifically, yellow to orange to red; having this quality in any color mixture

whole-to-part—characterized by an initial separation of the whole ABC before the parts, resulting from a defined silhouette or an overall surface treatment

References

Armstrong, Robert P. *The Affecting Presence.*
Urbana: Univ. of Illinois Press, 1971.

Arnheim, Rudolph. *Art and Visual Perception.* Berkeley: Univ. of California Press, 1974.

_____. *The Power of the Center.* Berkeley: Univ. of California Press, 1982.

_____. *Toward a Psychology of Art.* Berkeley: Univ. of California Press, 1966.

_____. *Visual Thinking.* Berkeley: Univ. of California Press, 1969.

Banner, L. W. *American Beauty.* Chicago: Univ. of Chicago Press, 1983.

Barratt, Krome. *Logic and Design.* Westfield, N.J.: Eastview Editions, 1980.

Barthes, Roland. *The Fashion System.* New York: Hill and Wang, 1983.

Bartley, S. Howard. *Perception in Everyday Life.* New York: Harper and Row, 1972.

Berlyne, D. E. *Conflict, Arousal and Curiosity.* New York: John Wiley and Sons, 1960.

_____. *Studies in the New Experimental Aesthetics.* New York: John Wiley and Sons, 1974.

Bloomer, Carolyn. *Principles of Visual Perception.* New York: Van Nostrand Reinhold Co., 1976.

Brockman, Helen. *The Theory of Fashion Design.* New York: John Wiley and Sons, 1965.

Collier, Graham. *Form, Space, and Vision.* Englewood Cliffs, N.J.: Prentice-Hall, 1967.

Csikszentmihalyi, Mihaly, and Rochberg-Halton, Eugene. *The Meaning of Things.* Cambridge: Cambridge Univ. Press, 1981.

Davis, Marian L. *Visual Design in Dress.* Englewood Cliffs, N.J.: Prentice-Hall, 1980.

DeLong, M. R. "Clothing and Aesthetics: Perception of Form," *Home Economics Research Journal* 47 (1978): 214–24.

DeLong, M. R., and Larntz, K. "Measuring Visual Response to Clothing," *Home Economics Research Journal* 8 (1980): 281–93.

DeLong, M. R., Salusso-Deonier, C., and Larntz, K. "Use of Perceptions of Female Dress as an Indicator of Role Definition," *Home Economics Research Journal* 11 (1983): 327–36.

Dondis, Donis. *A Primer of Visual Literacy.* Cambridge: MIT Press, 1973.

Eisner, Elliot. *Educating Artistic Vision.* New York: Macmillan Co., 1972.

Ellis, W. D. *A Sourcebook of Gestalt Psychology.* New York: Humanities Press, 1955.

Feldman, Edmund. *Art as Image and Idea.* Englewood Cliffs, N.J.: Prentice-Hall, 1967.

_____. *Varieties of Visual Experience.* New York: Harry Abrams, 1973.

Flugel, J. C. *The Psychology of Clothes.* New York: International Universities Press, 1969.

Forgus, R. H. *Perception.* New York: McGraw-Hill, 1966.

Fraser, Kennedy. *The Fashionable Mind.* New York: Alfred Knopf, 1981.

Gardner, Howard. *The Arts and Human Development.* New York: John Wiley and Sons, 1973.

Gibson, James J. *The Perception of the Visual World.* Westport, Conn.: Greenwood Press, 1950.

_____. *The Senses Considered as Perceptual Systems.* Boston: Houghton Mifflin, 1966.

Gombrich, E. H. *The Sense of Order.* Ithaca: Cornell Univ. Press, 1979.

Goodman, N. *Languages of Art.* Indianapolis: Hackett Publishing, 1976.

Hillestad, R. "The Underlying Structure of Appearance," *Dress* 5 (1980): 117–25.

Hollander, Anne. *Seeing Through Clothes.* New York: Viking Press, 1978.

Itten, Johannes. *The Elements of Color.* New York: Van Nostrand Reinhold Co., 1970.

Kaiser, S. B. *The Social Psychology of Clothing*. New York: Macmillan Co., 1985.

Kaufman, Lloyd. *Sight and Mind*. New York: Oxford Univ. Press, 1974.

Kepes, Gyorgy. *Language of Vision*. Chicago: Paul Theobalk and Co., 1969.

Kroeber, A. L. *Style and Civilizations*. Ithaca: Cornell Univ. Press, 1957.

Kubler, George. *The Shape of Time*. London: Yale Univ. Press, 1962.

Langer, Susanne K. *Feeling and Form*. New York: Charles Scribner's Sons, 1953.

Lowenfeld, V., and Brittain, W. L. *Creative and Mental Growth*. New York: Macmillan Co., 1964.

McKim, Robert. *Thinking Visually*. Belmont, Calif.: Wadsworth, 1980.

Martin, F. D. *Sculpture and Enlivened Space*. Lexington: Univ. Press of Kentucky, 1981.

Morton, G. M. *The Arts of Costume and Personal Appearance*. New York: John Wiley and Sons, 1964.

Munro, Thomas. *Form and Style in the Arts*. Cleveland: Press of Case Western Reserve Univ., 1970.

————. *Toward Science in Aesthetics*. NY: Liberal Arts Press, 1956.

Munsell Book of Color, Neighboring Hues Edition. Newburgh, N.Y.: Munsell Color Co., 1973.

Parmenter, Ross. *The Awakened Eye*. Middletown, Conn.: Wesleyan Univ. Press, 1968.

Peckham, Morse. *Man's Rage for Chaos*. New York: Schocken Books, 1965.

Pepper, S. *Principles of Art Appreciation*. New York: Harcourt Brace, 1949.

Roach, M. E., and Eicher, J. B. *The Visible Self: Perspectives on Dress*. Englewood Cliffs, N.J.: Prentice-Hall, 1973.

Rothschild, Lincoln. *Style in Art*. New York: Thomas Yoseloff, 1960.

Scott, Robert G. *Design Fundamentals*. New York: McGraw-Hill, 1951.

Smith, Ralph, ed. *Aesthetics and Problems of Education*. Urbana: Univ. of Illinois Press, 1971.

Stolnitz, Jerome. *Aesthetics and Philosophy of Art Criticism*. Cambridge, Mass.: Riverside Press, 1960.

Thiel, Philip. *Visual Awareness and Design*. Seattle: Univ. of Washington Press, 1981.

Wolfflin, H. *Principles of Art History*. New York: Henry Holt, 1932.

Yochim, L. D. *Perceptual Growth in Creativity*. Scranton, Pa.: International Textbook Co., 1967.

Zajonc, R. B. "Feeling and Thinking: Preferences Need No Inferences," *American Psychologist* 35 (1980):151–75.

Zajonc, R. B., and Markus, H. "Affective and Cognitive Factors in Preferences," *Journal of Consumer Research* 9 (1982):123–31.

Index

Gradation, 18–19, 15, 125
Grain, 60
Gravity, 40, 47, 60, 61
Gray, shades of, 92–93
Ground, 28. *See also* Figure-ground relation
Grounding, 46
Grouping, 18, 21, 72, 79, 97, 99, 100, 101, 102–3, 105, 107, 108–110, 112, 115, 124, 129

Habit, viewing, 7–8, 36, 64, 77, 108, 124, 155
Hand, 61–63, 70
Head, as focal point, 36–37
Head length, 37, 51
Hemline, 76, 101
Hierarchy, 79, 103, 107, 131
Horizontal line, 77, 126–27
Hue, 92, 113

Identification, of ABC, 135
Imagination, 159–60
Indeterminate surface, 33–35
Individuality, of shape, 132
Inferred relation, 21
Integration, 28, 97, 124–26
Intensity, of color, 93, 113
Interaction, 17, 52, 58, 65–70, 80, 86, 95, 102
Interdependence, 124–25
Interpretation, of ABC, 14, 16, 115–49, 151, 153

Kinesthetic experience, 69

Language, for systematic analysis. *See* Vocabulary
Layout, 52, 59–64, 67, 85, 112
Length, of line, 74–75
Level, visual, 108, 129
Light and shadow, 52, 64–65, 68
Lighting, 65, 68
Limbs, 37–38, 44–45
Line, 72, 73–80, 113, 122
Locomotion. *See* Movement
Logic and Design, 102
Look, 133–34

Material, 52–71
Meaning, 142–43. *See also*

Association
Merit, visual, 16
Message, 16, 141–42, 160
Methodology, 3
Microlayout, 88
Modifier, 102–14
Movement, 24, 26
  body, 39–40, 47, 104
  impression of, 103
Munsell Book of Color, Neighboring Hues Edition, 51

Number, 102–3

Objectivity, 7, 10, 13, 151, 153–54
Observation, 14–15, 152. *See also* Viewing
Order, 54, 116–17, 120
  pattern of, 129
Ordering, sequential, 131
Organization
  of ABC, 35, 36, 71, 97, 98–102, 115–32, 135
  side-by-side, 129–30
Outline, 81, 83

Part. *See* Visual part
Part-to-whole relation, 97–114, 119, 131
Pattern, 55–57, 81, 85–86, 103, 112, 116
  of ABC, 140
  regional, 147
Perception, 3–7, 23–24, 93–94, 99, 108, 115, 130, 155, 156
  analytical, 5–7. *See also* Systematic analysis
  casual, 5
Perception of the Visual World, 23
Perspective, 7, 23–24, 40–42
Photographs, use of, in systematic analysis, 10–12, 14
Photography, 20, 110
Pigment, 78–79. *See also* Color
Pile, 89
Planar relation, 29
  integration, 28–31
  separation, 28–31
Pleat, 78
Point, 86–87, 122
Position
  of line, 77

of shape, 84
  spatial, 89, 94, 108
Predictability, 139–41
Preference, 3, 157
Priority, viewing, 16, 21, 24–35, 46, 49–50, 57–58, 80, 81, 86, 87, 91, 95, 99, 103, 115, 116, 121–23, 127, 128
Professionalism, 151–61
Proportion, 106
Proximity, 100–101
Purpose, 118

Quality, 157

Randomness, 129, 131–32
Range, 8, 120, 139
Relationships. *See* Visual relations
Repetition, 103, 104–5, 125
Reversal, 30
Rhythm, 104

Scanning, 22–23, 99, 103, 105, 115, 116, 126
Seamline, 61, 66, 77
Seeing, 3
Segregation, 18, 21, 41–42, 46, 72, 97, 99, 106, 112, 115, 129
Sensory attributes, 18–19
Separates, 28
Separation, 26, 28, 124. *See also* Segregation
Sequence, temporal, 128
Shade, 92
Shadow, 52, 64–65, 68
Shape
  depth, 83
  planar, 83
  simple to complex, 82
Shoulders, 38
Silhouette, 20, 24–28, 31, 60, 61, 82, 84–85, 86
Similarity, 98–99, 120, 124, 125, 129, 136
Situation, 5–6, 143, 154–55
Size, 105–6
Space, 5–6, 19–20, 22–35, 116
  negative. *See* Ground
  positive. *See* Figure
  use of
    closed or open, 24–26
    determinate or
      indeterminate, 33–35
    flat or rounded, 31–33
    planar separation or

integration, 28–31
whole or part, 26–28
Stability, of visual relationships, 102, 120
Strength, 137
Structuring, visual
layout, 59–64
shadow, 64–65
surface, 53–59
Subjectivity, 153–54
Subtlety, 128–29, 133–34, 139–40
Surface, 31–35, 87–95, 110
body, 44, 45
structure of, 52, 53–59, 63–64
Surprise, 139–41
Surround, 22, 99
Symbol, 136
Symmetry, 38, 43, 103
bilateral, 107
Systematic analysis, 13–21, 95, 127–28

Tactile quality, 63, 69
Texture, 87–91, 113
Theme, 139

Theory of Fashion Design, The, 63
Thickness, of surface, 33, 55,
Three-dimensional shape, 83–84, 104
Time, 146–47, 148
Tint, 92
Torso, 37, 44
Tradition, 144, 156–57
Transformation, of material, 61, 62, 66–67
Transition, 125–26
Transparency, 54, 100, 101

Undertone, 93
Unit and interval, 103

Value, 65, 91, 92–93, 113
Value judgment, 14
Verticality, 77, 126
Viewer, 6, 10
casual, 151, 155–58
role of, 13, 36, 41–42, 95, 97, 115, 116, 120, 123–24, 142–43, 151–61
Viewing, 13–21

simultaneous, 130–31
successive, 131
sustained, 115
Viewing order, 128
Viewing path, 126–27
Viewing tempo, 129
Visual field, 22–24
Visual function
of color, 91–92
of line, 73
of point, 86
of shape, 80
Visual literacy, 3, 6
Visual part, 97–114, 115, 130, 131
Visual path, 26, 126–27
Visual relations, 15, 17–21
Visual response, 5–7
Visual weight, 106
Visual world, 22
Vocabulary, 9–10, 13, 14, 34

Weave, 88
Weight
of fabric, 47, 61
ʼvisual, 107–10
Workmanship, 157–58